'The Rev. Jackie Ross has been a principled, doughty and determined devotee to his cause. And what a worthy cause it is too! We will probably never know just how many individual lives, families and communities within Europe particularly, have been touched by his sterling work.

The great thing is that it is not just the recipients who have benefited from the contribution of Blythswood; the givers have experienced the glow of knowing that their efforts are making a direct humanitarian contribution.

To achieve all this from a base in South-west Ross is even more remarkable. I salute this talented and tenacious man of such good will and positive achievement.

Rt Hon. Charles Kennedy
Leader of Liberal Democratic Party

This book traces Jackie Ross's life from its roots in Easter Ross to rural Wester Ross and that might have been the extent of his influence had Jackie not been burdened for the world. Converted as a young man, Jackie has never been afraid to stand up for Christ. His character, his life and his work all demonstrate what God can do in a man and through him. And his raw enthusiasm in pushing forward and pioneering work in areas where many would fear to tread has challenged me to the core.

Blythswood and Jackie Ross are inseparable, but the focus of the book is Jackie. It provides fascinating insights into his personal and family life and into his ministry in Lochcarron and his involvement in that small community. But it does more that that. It lets us look into the heart of a man who knows he is dying and whose trust for time and eternity is firmly fixed on the Lord Jesus Christ.

We in Open Door Trust Glasgow owe a debt of gratitude to Jackie Ross, and so will everyone who reads this book.

Maureen McKenna, Author
Founder of Open Doors Trust, Glasgow

This is a fascinating account of a life in the Highlands of Scotland devoted to the care of soul and body of a huge variety of people. Although that work has been carried on in recent years mainly through Blythswood Care, with material and spiritual help going out to many parts of the world, it started at home. Narrated through the words of Rev. Jackie Ross himself, of his children and their spouses, of his own family, and of his wife Elma and her sister, as well as of some of those who have worked closely with him, it is a frank insight into what made Jackie tick – a deep love for Christ and a warm wish that all he meets should know that love.

I have known Jackie from his youth, when I was privileged to know his late father, sometimes being delighted to accompany him when he drove a grocery van for Kenneth Matheson, Dingwall, and I am grateful that this book will share that knowledge with all who read it.

Lord Mackay of Clashfern

Outstanding Christian men like Jackie Ross have no idea why the rest of us respect, admire and love them – but this book goes a long way to providing the explanation. For here is the story of a loveable, dedicated, wonderfully human, and – yes – at times frustrated and frustrating, man. These pages are full of important lessons: vision for extending Christ's kingdom does not depend on the size of your city, but on the size of your love; simple, disciplined family life can be immensely happy; eccentricity and fruitful Christian service are not mutually exclusive; seriousness and fun are not opposites. On top of all this, An Irregular Candidate is simply a great read; your whole family will love it!

Sinclair B Ferguson
St George's Tron, Church of Scotland, Glasgow

AN IRREGULAR CANDIDATE

JACKIE ROSS OF BLYTHSWOOD

IRENE HOWAT

CHRISTIAN FOCUS

Psalm quotations at the beginning of each
chapter are taken from the 1650 Metrical Psalter

ISBN 1-85792-742-7

Copyright © Christian Focus Publications

Published in 2002
by
Christian Focus Publications, Geanies House,
Fearn, Ross-shire, IV20 1TW, Scotland.

www.christianfocus.com

Cover Design by Alister MacInnes

Printed and bound by
WS Bookwell, Finland

Contents

Preface

Why agree to co-operate in writing a book about myself? There are many reasons why the servant of Christ should think twice, not least because the only judgement that counts is the Lord's. Only he can disclose the motives of men's hearts (1 Cor 4:1-5). It is also true that Christian biographies can be used to advance sectarianism or become a substitute for genuine interest in God's Word. But I have agreed to do this because I consider it a wonderful opportunity to say to people, 'Thank you,' and, 'Sorry, please forgive me.' In a public way I can also say to God, 'Thank you for forgiving me and allowing me to serve you.'

This life of mine has been an experience of discovering that God is gracious and forgiving in restoring backsliders and giving us work to do. That was the experience of David the Psalmist and the Apostle Peter. Although trapped and paralysed by sin, the Lord Jesus brought Peter to repentance and to say 'Lord, you know all things; you know that I love you.' And he gave him more work to do. Certainly, God has done this for me more than once.

Because written by a friend, contributed to by friends and family, and published by friends, this book does not publicise my faults. Nevertheless faults I do have. To those to whom I have failed to listen, whom I have pressurised, of whose generosity and goodwill I have taken advantage, I say, 'Sorry.' If my behaviour has ever disaffected some towards the Gospel and the Lord Jesus Christ, I ask you not to refuse the Gospel because of the messenger.

To my mentors in the Free Presbyterian Church, Associated Presbyterian Churches, and many other Christian friends who directed, corrected, and encouraged me I say, 'Thank you.'

Christian publishers, missions, aid organisations and businesses of all kinds, including bankers, have supported Blythswood along the way. As Donald Macaskill, my brother-in-law and former director of John G Eccles Printers says, 'Being Christians, we were delighted to print for Blythswood and payment was a secondary matter. Jackie was thrilled and took full advantage of it.' This will ring true for many of you. I apologise and ask for forgiveness. It was not done thoughtlessly, but knowingly, and that makes it worse. What amazes me is that you are more involved with Blythswood than ever. Thank you and, above all, thanks to God.

Trustees of Blythswood, staff, volunteers, and all supporters, past and present – for your forbearance, prayerful giving, hard work and dependability I thank God, and you.

Being terminally ill with cancer has made me aware of the love of the extended family which in some cases extends to four generations. Our five children with their husbands and wives, along with their children, have given me great joy and happiness. I now understand my own grandmother being a little upset with my father praying for us as if we were sinners! My prayer is that the youngest grandchild to the oldest in the extended family would know the great blessing of forgiveness of sin and peace with God.

To Elma, my wife, and mother of our five children, I say, 'Thanks for your love and forbearance in the past. Thank you especially for fulfilling your marriage vow to love in sickness and in health until death parts us. That is like Christ who loved and cared for us when we could not care for ourselves. We along with multitudes will be more like him yet. 'We know that when he appears, we shall be like him, for we shall see him as is' 1 John 3:2.

Jackie Ross
January 2002

Introduction

I had never met Jackie Ross until I started working on this book. I knew a good deal about him, about his ministry in Lochcarron, his years of work through Blythswood and the fact that he was suffering from terminal cancer. But none of that prepared me to meet Jackie. No-one had told me that he was a man of great passion, who would shed tears as we talked of his childhood home, of conversions in his family and through his ministry. Nor was I prepared for his sensitivity and gentleness. He was more concerned about me than about his own pain. And I certainly was not prepared to research a book about a man who didn't want to talk about himself. Jackie waxed eloquent about family and congregational matters, he spoke sadly about difficult times and enthused about Blythswood. But getting him to talk about himself was very hard work. Consequently, I had to research my subject elsewhere. Thankfully, Jackie comes from a family of nine, and he and Elma produced five children of their own. They, along with Elma, were rich sources of material, as were a number of their friends, some of the people of Lochcarron and Jackie's colleagues in Blythswood. I'm grateful to them for their help.

Because so much of the material in this book comes from people other than Jackie, the contributors require some introduction. Jackie has four brothers and four sisters. His brothers are Neil, who is married to Gena, Donald to Catherine, Edward to Stevie and John is married to Morag. They are all Rosses. Then there are his sisters. Catherine is married to Calum MacInnes, Sheena to Sam Grant, Marion to Bill Byers and Margo to Donald Macaskill. In the text his brothers and sisters are referred to by their Christian names, his brothers-in-law by their full names the first time they appear in each chapter, then by Christian names thereafter. Elma has one sister, Kathmar Campbell. She is married to George. Jackie and Elma's children have shared memories, both happy and sad. Throughout the book Philip, Sarah, Lois, Jeremy and Jason are known by their Christian names only. Other contributors are introduced in the text. I'm grateful to every one of them. Material which has been contributed has been indented in the text. The rest is Jackie's story as he told it to me.

This book was written while Jackie was suffering from what proved to be terminal cancer. Jackie passed away on the 13th March 2002 and since his death 2 final pieces were added to the book, chapter 14 was written by his son Philip and also added was Jackie's last letter.

Jackie and Elma welcomed me into their hearts at a time when that must have been far from easy. I am unable to thank them adequately for that privilege.

Irene Howat

Acknowledgments

This book could not have been written without the help of many people. As well as thanking Jackie's family I should like to express my gratitude to Martin Cameron, James Campbell, Kathmar Campbell, Mairi Forsyth, James MacDonald, Christabel Mackay, Maureen McKenna, Finlay MacKenzie, Ishbel Mackinnon, Geraldine Maclennan, Helen Murchison, David Murray, Christian Puritz, Frank Rennie, Donald and Alison Stewart, John O. Sutherland, Anne Tallach, John Tallach, Anne Todd, Donald MacLeod, Levente Horváth, Cornel Iova, Arjen van Kralingen, and Jan van Woerden.

1

O children, hither do ye come,
and unto me give ear;
I shall you teach to understand
how ye the Lord should fear
(Psalm 34:11)

Childhood in Ross-shire

I had a dream for my future. I'd be a crofter, maybe
even run a small farm. My days would be spent caring
for sheep and a few cows and tinkering with my Fergie
tractor. It was going to be a grey tractor. And another
part of my dream was in colour, for my wife was to
have red hair. In the dream my red-headed wife was at
home with our big family of children. There was a lot
of laughter in the house, the smell of baking, toys
scattered on the floor, and a happy buzz about the place.
My wife was a good woman, training the children in
the Christian faith and leaving me free to enjoy myself.
And at thirteen years of age, in order to make that dream
begin to come true, I left part of it behind. That was

when I left home to go to agricultural school sixty miles away at Balmacara. And the part I left behind was the houseful of children and the laughter and the busyness. And I missed them more than I had words to describe.

My father came from Kildary in Easter Ross, and when he left school he went to work at Munro's of Invergordon, Engineers, to train as a mechanic, and later to Clashnessie near Lochinver where he met Mam. After they were married they moved back to Kildary where Dad worked in a grocer's shop. My older brother, Neil, and I were born there. Before long Dad went to Conon Bridge to work a grocery van for Kenneth Matheson, Grocer, of Dingwall. Some more of the family of nine were born there. Just before the outbreak of the Second World War we moved to Ferintosh where the remainder of the family was born and where I spent my childhood. And what an exciting place it was. During the first year of the war there were soldiers with mules camped in the woods around us. My imagination ran riot and time passed in a succession of exciting games. Not all of them pleased Mam, such as when I gave household things to some soldiers in exchange for chocolate!

We were about a mile from school and Mam sent us there each morning with a packed lunch which was intended to last us the day. But my friend, James, and I knew differently. After we'd finished our packed lunch in the playground, we'd run off down the road for home where Mam would feed us with pancakes; then we would pelt back up the road in time for afternoon class. Nothing seemed to faze our mother, even the births of her children. I remember when two of the younger members of the family were born. We went off to school as usual in the morning, Mam waving to us from the door, and when we came back there was a new baby. Because babies were then delivered at home with a midwife in attendance, I thought that they came in the black bag the midwife carried around with her!

There were many people in the countryside when I was young. Farms were labour intensive, families were bigger than they are today, and added to that were other children who were boarded in the area for several years during the war. One evacuee provided us with a nature study lesson that I remember to this day. Robert was a city boy and the simple pleasures of country life fascinated him. One day he came into our kitchen to show Mam his latest treasure, a small frog. Mam, who was beating a pancake batter, stopped to admire the creature, and as she did so it jumped from Robert's hand and landed in the bowl of batter. And the lesson we learned was this: frogs can swim in pancake batter as well as they can in water. Robert fished it out and I can't remember what Mam did with the batter, but I have a suspicion that it was judged to be none the worse for its visitor and we had pancakes for tea.

Marion

Ours was a happy home. We all ran free and wild in the countryside around our home. Although there was plenty of mischief we knew right from wrong from our earliest days. We were never in any doubt about what we should and shouldn't do. But there was no fear in the discipline of our home. If we did wrong the distress we caused Dad was more salutary, than any row he could have given us. My memories of Mam are that she seemed to work endlessly, as no doubt she had to. We were not well off, but there was always something on the table. So far as I remember we lacked for nothing, though in summer, like everyone else around us we didn't wear shoes. We were well taught at home both in Scripture and Catechism. In family worship we read round the family, one verse each, starting as soon as we could read. And, contrary to what people think of a Christian Highland Sunday, we enjoyed ourselves. We liked going to church and we liked the way our parents spent the day with us. We used to line up at the window and sing psalms and hymns, and we sang so loudly that people out on the road could hear us.

There were always children about the place, Mam seemed to have a never ending supply of scones, pancakes and home-made rhubarb jam. Sometimes there would be fifteen or sixteen children in the house. As well as being full of children, most of the time our home was full of laughter. Mam had a great sense of fun, and she always seemed to be laughing with us or at our antics. Because she spoke Gaelic and my father did not, she used to tease him using words he only half understood.

The war being fought in Europe affected even our country lives in Ross-shire, because the government encouraged crofters to make the best use of their land to help the war effort. We lived in a cottage in five acres of whin, bracken, and moorland. Dad, who was unfit for full military service because he had lost two fingers in an accident, got a Department of Agriculture tractor, and we ploughed the land and transformed it into a market garden. We were all involved in the work, even the smallest one could pick strawberries and the like. Dad also kept hens and we sold what eggs were left after the family's needs had been met. I loved working with Dad, especially when other men came along to help. Their discussions fascinated me. Christianity often seemed to be the topic tackled and I listened as they debated. There was something of quiet certainty in Dad. He wasn't a forceful man, far from it, but there couldn't have been a man in the neighbourhood who didn't know Dad's mind on the matter. Digging for victory wasn't the only thing Dad did for crown and country. He was a member of the Home Guard and I can still remember my feeling of pride as I watched him go out on duty on his bicycle, to keep the Germans back. On his back he carried a .303 rifle with no ammunition of any kind in it. I felt safe when I knew my father was guarding the land. Mam must have enjoyed our pleasure in Dad, for her own father died before she was born.

There was another side to my father that fascinated me – he was an inventor. How things worked fascinated him, and at least twice he took things through from first principles to finished product and tried to get patents. He tackled these projects in a very organised way, starting off with drawings and then moving to working models. Had Dad been born half a century later, he might well have played a part in the great technological revolution.

Dad bore testimony to his faith in his daily life, both in how he lived and what he said, and his main concern for his family was that they would put their faith in Jesus. Sunday by Sunday, we were questioned on what we'd heard in church – I suppose Dad was catechising us, but it seemed like a quiz to me. God was part of our family life, even to the point of confusion in my case. We had relations in Dunfermline who sent us their children's outgrown clothing. But I thought that the clothes came directly from God because my father was so full of prayerful thanks for them! There was no separation between what was Christian and secular in our family life except that on a Sunday the focus was on what was Christian.

Sundays were special, and they were busy. We were up quite early to feed the hens before getting ready for church. We went to the local Free Church in the mornings and in the evenings walked for an hour and a half to Dingwall Free Presbyterian Church. One Sunday evening we went to a service in Ferintosh Public Hall. As we walked home afterwards I overheard Mam and the minister's wife talking. They were discussing the fact that the hens were off the lay! I spent the rest of the walk wondering why they were talking about a weekday thing on a Sunday. I suppose at that time I was going through one of my bouts of trying to win God's favour by trying to be very spiritual. Although we were brought up to keep God's day special, Sundays were not dismal. They were real family days and I, for one, enjoyed them. There were things we didn't do on Sundays, like read secular books, but mostly there wasn't time anyway because the day was so full. But I do remember one occasion when I wished things were different. I was reading my first big book – it was on motor racing – and I didn't quite finish it on a Saturday night. I wished I could read it the following day but, having been brought up under the text, 'Thou, God, seest me,' I was afraid to creep away and read it. In fact, that text regularly stopped me from doing certain things because it stuck in my mind. That's not to say that I was perfect, far from it, but without such reminders of the Lord I would have been involved in things that would have only led me into deeper sin. Indeed, at times I had such a desire to please myself and do wrong that I would shut my mind to, 'Thou, God, seest me.' But now one of my greatest comforts is that God sees all and knows all, and that, however sinful my thoughts and acts may be, his forgiveness is full and complete.

Margo
We lived in the country and I have many happy memories of childhood spent playing in the wooded areas and moors, and among the heather and bracken. It was wonderful for imaginative games, and there was no shortage of these. All of this carefree, untroubled childhood was surrounded by loving parents whose main aim was to see all their children come to know Christ. Naughtiness was punished and, there being nine of us, no doubt my father and mother were sad on many occasions. We got up to many pranks and the house always seemed to be invaded by other children. Children attract children and I suppose that is what happened in

our home. Many are the memories of my father gathering us all around and teaching us Bible truths, praying with us and for us. On occasions he would call us in from our play and send us all to our bedrooms to pray, such was his concern for us. My father used to get us to take notes of the sermons and I remember him taking our notes and giving them to the minister to read. We attended two churches, one beside us and the other some miles away. Both ministers were very kind to my family. When Mr Macfarlane, the minister from Dingwall, visited us I well remember that when we saw his car come along the road we would stop our game and see who would be first to meet him – this included the local children. We would all then pile into the sitting room and sit there panting and puffing, waiting for him to read God's Word and pray for us.

When I was aged ten or eleven, one of my teachers called into question the existence of God. Part of the curriculum was basic horticulture. When we were working in the garden we were shown how shooting a fine spray of water with a stirrup pump could form part of a rainbow. This ability to make a rainbow was used as evidence that the wonders of nature had no need of a divine creator and that there was in fact no God. That disturbed and frightened me. That night I told my parents what had happened and, by the time we had finished discussing the issue, I was more confident than ever that there was a God. I well remember my father's response to the incident – it was one of sorrow that we should have been so misled. And his sorrow overrode any anger he might have felt at such an abuse of trust. Dad's reaction was to me a proof of the existence of God. Some years ago I conducted a funeral at which that teacher was present. It was a strange providence that I should have had the occasion to witness about the Lord to the very one who tried to tell me that God didn't even exist, and to see that person visibly moved by what was said.

Coming from a Christian home didn't set us apart at school because in those days most folk had a church connection and in our area the Free Church was particularly strong. In the homes of several of my friends, family worship was conducted, as it was in my own. And the influence even extended to surprising places. For some it was no more than a formal habit, but it was a good one and the effects of frequent reading of God's Word were seen later in their lives.

During the winter of my first year at Muir-of-Ord Junior Secondary School there was a heavy fall of snow. It fell thick and fast and the hours in school dragged. No subject could hold my attention that day. I could hardly wait for the school bus to drop me off at Ferintosh Primary School where I had left my bicycle. My mind raced ahead to hiding behind a big rock, piling up snowballs to pelt at others as they passed by. Even the chores I knew I had to do took on new delights at the prospect of ploughing though the snow to do them. And these things might all have happened had I not been so keen to get on with them. Taking no thought for traffic – there was little enough of it in those days anyway – I pedalled like mad out of the school gate on to the road and was struck by a car. I suffered head injuries and was about a month off school during which I wasn't well enough to enjoy the rest of that winter's snow. But I was well enough to think, and the accident did make me think. 'What would have happened if I had died?' I wondered. And I knew that was on Dad's mind too. In his anxiety about the souls of his children, he used this opportunity to impress on us the fact that not everyone grew to a ripe old age before meeting their Maker.

The driver of the car got a terrible shock and he came to see how I was. When I had recovered from my injuries he brought me a present – a pony! And it was the most wicked animal on the face of the earth. Going behind him was guaranteed to provoke him to kicking both hind legs straight out in my direction. When he was gracious enough to allow me to get on his back, he went off like a shot and I had to hang on for dear life. Then one day, when he went for the world speed record, I left his back for the last time, when he went under a high fence. He went straight back to his owner that day and I wasn't sorry to see the back of him!

That was all behind me as I left for the sixty mile trip to Balmacara. As the noise of the family's goodbyes faded, in manly fashion I tried to fight back the tears and my heart felt like a heavy stone inside me.

2

By what means shall a young man learn
his way to purify?
If he according to thy word
thereto attentive be.
(Psalm 119:9)

Growing Years

Arriving at Balmacara did nothing to ease my homesickness. At the beginning of what I saw as my life as a farmer, though something in me was excited at being away from home, I was miserable. Leaving the happy atmosphere that was home was like leaving part of my inside behind. There was a real and palpable emptiness and never in my two years at Balmacara did it really go away. I remember looking at a map and working out the route to walk home. But it was sixty miles, and so many lochs seemed to be in the way. Strange things gave me comfort, like being taken to church by the Gollan family who welcomed me into their Plockton home. Although their children had left home there were other young people there and the conversation was much like home. Just getting back into the kind of atmosphere I was used to helped in one way though it sharpened my homesickness in another. And letters from home made me feel I was amputated from what meant most to me. One letter from my father shows how he felt, and that his concern for me was much deeper than just hoping that I was well settled at school.

'My dear Jackie,

Just a short line in reply to your letter. We are glad you are well and enjoy being there. We are all well but Edward was out of school with a nail hole in his foot. He is better tonight. We are just after reading. All now in bed but Neil is also writing you. We have finished twelve nest boxes, but there is a lot to do. Tell me in your next letter are you far from Shiel Bridge or not.

Well my dear Jackie, I am missing you very much and so also are the others. I did not realise how much you filled a part of my life. We had a very enjoyable Sunday with questions and answers. I wished you were with us but I am glad you are happy there. Have confidence in Christ and what he did for us at Calvary. Edward asked some peculiar question but we got him put right and indeed it was all very edifying.

Remember your prayers and like things you were taught here at home. Remember Christ who is all things to you that are good for you and who gave his all for you. Keep always remembering him. Talk often to him. Tell him all your sins and your troubles. Remember he died for you. He is your best and most powerful friend, Jackie. Draw near to him, Jackie, and he will draw near to you my boy. Till the eternal day dawn and the shadows flee away Jackie, try harder and harder to draw near to him who desires your salvation so much that he died for you.

I hope you will get on well.

With love,

from Dad.'[1]

I found myself with two very different headmasters at Balmacara. The first made no impression on me for good or ill in terms of the Christian faith, but the second one certainly did. John O. Sutherland was a man of firm beliefs and unyielding principles. He brought a strong spiritual emphasis into the whole school. And it was he who reinforced the ecumenical aspect of my life. Although we sometimes attended the Free Church, we were Free Presbyterians. John O. Sutherland encouraged me to attend the Free Church and the Church of Scotland as well. In fact, he reminded me just as my father did that I should fix my eyes on Jesus. John O. Sutherland's influence did not cease when I left school. He continued to be interested in what I was doing and encouraged me to keep on at it.

John O. Sutherland

The passage of time so often clouds the vision and in no case more so than to recall a chapter in life which takes me back half a century. I had just embarked on my first headship and met a challenge

1. See pages 200-1 for the original hand-written letter from Jackie's dad

which exceeded my expectations. Not only had I moved to a different part of the country but I had moved to a desk where the buck stopped. I was confronted with a group of boys who were total strangers to me, who knew each other, but who did not know me. I knew they were assessing me, indeed I became the centrepiece of their discussion. The only thing I knew about them was that they, like all other boys, were sure to try me out. At least that was not a new problem!

When I arrived in Balmacara I was faced with an amorphous situation into which I was compelled to bring a degree of organisation. As I had come from a school where order was the norm, I moved quickly to establish such a pattern but soon realised that I had to start from scratch. I consulted the staff who were helpful but not all that unanimous in their opinions. My instinct for action was derived from reports that there were often confrontations between boys from the islands, the east and the west, and I saw a means of thwarting this by creating school houses with a complete mix, and laying down the rule that loyalty to the house was the honourable rule which had to be paramount. So far so good. At least it gave the boys a new subject for discussion.

To implement my plan I required leaders. The staff knew the sportsmen, the bullies and the trouble makers. I wanted trouble shooters. I decided on a ballot of each house to elect a captain and vice-captain and I would reserve the right to choose a school captain. It was a gamble that paid off. I can't remember who were all elected but this was the first time I came face to face with Jackie Ross.

He had been easily elected captain of his house. He was bright and breezy, always in good form, not afraid to take decisions and take the rap if need be. He was said to be typical of the *Tom Brown's Schooldays* character whose ears, it was alleged, could be boxed, rightly or wrongly, in the morning, because he was sure to merit it later in the day. Jackie was a born leader. He and his fellow captains, Peter MacLean and Donald Macaulay, were a very successful trio who displayed leadership and loyalty as well as effective discipline. I have never forgotten them.

Even fifty years ago moral and spiritual values were beginning to slip, and it was necessary to give a firm lead. Boys from church-going homes invariably responded, others acquiesced, few rebelled. It was easy to see that Jackie had been well brought up. I only had him for about six months when he left for the wider world, but he always kept up and, like so many, came back to visit. When faced with his father's death at an early age, he took over the business, and in the course of his travels he appeared on my doorstep with his van. He was astute enough to be making a social call, and stayed the night. Jackie knew how to survive! Thereafter I followed his career with interest and was not surprised at some of his escapades. My last encounter with Jackie, in his bachelor days, was on a train in the company of three of his brothers. I seem to recall that they were all divinity students. It was a heart-warming experience. But his crowning achievement was his discernment to choose a bride from the Clan Sutherland. I say no more!

Although being away from home made me do a bit of growing up, a holiday at home from Balmacara reminded me that in my parents' eyes I was still a boy. It was threshing time at the local farm and there was so much to see. I was up and off in the mornings to watch the goings on. And when the threshing mill arrived, pulled by a steam engine, my excitement could hardly be contained. One day the men worked at the mill till late at night, and I stayed on past my bedtime, far too interested in the men and the machinery to drag myself away. And what a row awaited me when I eventually trailed home, the dust of the mill hanging on me. They thought I deserved it for my thoughtlessness and disobedience. And they were right.

Catherine

We used to look forward to Jackie coming home from Balmacara on holiday because we missed him greatly. On Sunday evenings we would sit in front of the fire and sing psalms and hymns. If we picked one we had to start it. One night, after we had been singing together, we were about to go off to bed. I was last to go and only Dad, Mam, Jackie and I were in the kitchen. 'I learned a new hymn at school,' Jackie said. 'Why don't you sing it to us?' Dad asked. Jackie looked at me. 'I'll sing it if Catherine goes off to bed. She'll laugh at me.' Dad assured him that I wouldn't and so I stayed. Jackie began the first line of 'Yield not to Temptation' and I started to laugh. I was sent to bed instantly and quite right too!

After a couple of years away at school it was time to look for a job. Two were advertised in the *Ross-shire Journal*, one for a trainee draughtsman with a firm of architects and civil engineers and the other for an agricultural mechanic. I thought I could do either job but didn't know which one to go for. Technical drawing interested me, probably because of my father's fascination for knowing how things worked and for inventing things himself. But that wasn't what made up my mind which job to go for. It was much more mundane than that. The following Monday morning I awoke to a pouring wet day and the thought of spending my life up to my elbows in tractor engines in the rain didn't appeal to me at all. So in 1951, aged 15, I started my training as an architectural draughtsman. My first job was to work on building plans, watercolouring the work for the different tradesmen – it was on the plans for the Lochcarron Free Presbyterian Church manse though I had no way of knowing that it would one day be our home! At the time I remember thinking how awful it would be to live in a place like Lochcarron. Having been in Balmacara, not too far from Lochcarron for two years I reckoned, in the new found sophistication of being a working man, that it was a million miles from anywhere. How wrong I was!

Although Dad was mostly a cheerful man, from time to time he was unwell and I used to worry about what would happen if Dad didn't get better or if he didn't come home. And one day he didn't. Dad and one of my sisters were out in his grocery van – he was then fifty years old – going round the rural area from door to door, when he became suddenly very unwell. My sister took him away from the wheel and drove the van to a house. Help was sent for and Dad was taken to hospital in Dingwall where a cerebral haemorrhage was diagnosed. He was then transferred to Aberdeen, well over a hundred miles away. Because I took over the van when Dad went into hospital I was unable to visit him there.

Margo

Suddenly, amidst this happy childhood, disaster struck – my father took ill. I vividly remember the worry and fear even as a child of, 'What if Dad dies?' My father had a small grocer's business and he used to go out with a grocery van to all the country villages and houses. This meant long hours so it was a frequent occurrence to see my father come home late, tired and hungry, and my mother giving him his dinner at 10 o'clock at night. Then one night he did not arrive home and I remember as a twelve-year-old going to the window with my mother to watch for the lights of his van coming up the road. I remember asking God to bring him home.

At midnight an ambulance drew up at our house and my older sister got out. She had been helping my father that day with his grocery round. Dad had become ill and was taken into hospital. Three weeks later he died. I remember the tears and sadness in the house and wondering what would happen to us all. Children have their own way of coping with grief, and as long as things remain stable and secure they get over it. My mother and three older brothers provided that stability and security

for me and I suspect for my younger brother and
sister too.

I found it difficult to accept what had happened when
Dad died. At eighteen years old I felt I still needed him
and I simply couldn't believe he wasn't there for me.
Even when I saw his remains I couldn't take in the
finality of it all. It was a comfort to Mam to hear that
even when Dad was so ill in hospital he testified to
God's saving grace, singing Psalm 23 in his hospital
bed. And though I felt glad about that I was really in a
state of great confusion. We had experience of tragedy
before, when three of the children who used to come
to our home were drowned in a loch when they were
out collecting gulls eggs. But terrible though that had
been at the time, this was Dad, my dad, and I still needed
him. I went through a bad patch before I even began
to come to terms with losing my father, but I had to
get on with things as I was then the oldest son at home.
I left my job, took over the grocery van business and
tried to keep it going. But it didn't work out and I
returned to my draughtsmanship.

Catherine

Jackie has always been enterprising, even when he
was a boy. After Dad's death and while I was still at
school he got an old truck and used it to go round
the area selling firewood. One day I took my teacher
home – she had known Mam when they were
younger. As we walked down the path to the house
I saw Jackie at the truck. I was such a proud little
madam that I told her Jackie was helping another
guy sell firewood. There was no way I was going to

admit that the wreck belonged to our family. But my pride took a beating. Jackie strode out to meet us, and told my teacher all about his truck and his brilliant idea of selling firewood round the doors! Nothing has changed. Jackie's as enterprising now as he was then, and he's not too proud to get his hands dirty if it will help someone.

A year or two after Dad died, Mam took ill. As she seemed very unwell we called the doctor and he came to the house. Jackie took all of us who were at home into the kitchen. We stood there feeling sad and worried, until Jackie said, 'Let's pray the doctor will give Mam the right treatment.' He stood there with us and prayed. Next door the doctor gave Mam an injection that helped her, and within an hour she was obviously much better. That incident made a big impression on me. I saw prayer being answered almost immediately.

As I progressed through my apprenticeship I did some private work and the money it brought in allowed me to have a comfortable standard of living, which was helped, of course, by the fact that I was still staying at home. The whole family was involved in church life and at communion weekends and other times the house was full of the Lord's people. They were our friends. What interested us interested them too, and they were supportive of Mam in her widowhood and of my younger brothers and sisters, some of whom were still at school. Because my brother Neil, the oldest of the family, was in the RAF, much of the responsibility for the family fell on me, and I was therefore grateful for the support of our Christian friends. When my time came to do National Service I joined the RAF too. I was sent to London, to HQ Coastal Command, where I served as a teleprinter operator. There I discovered that though I thought I had grown up and could stand on my own two feet, I was every bit as homesick in London as I had been as a schoolboy in Balmacara.

Perhaps I'd feel the better of going to a SASRA meeting, I decided. But I didn't. I came out feeling very censorious about the whole thing, and in the darkness outside my billet I shared my thinking with a corporal who had been there too.

'John' he said, 'Are you trusting in Jesus yourself?'

It was like a bath of cold water to discover that he didn't join me in my criticism. Now I look on that as the providence of God for the corporal disappeared into the night and left me alone to work things out with the Lord.

Remembering the warmth of being with Christian people, I went along to the Free Presbyterian Church in London one Sunday some time afterwards.

'Are you saved?' Mr MacQueen, the minister, asked as we shook hands at the door.

'I'm seeking,' I told him.

He looked me in the eye. 'Seeking won't save you, only finding will.'

For me, seeking meant taking comfort in religious activities rather than in Christ, and perhaps that perceptive man knew the truth. I then went through a phase of trying to ensure I didn't do wrong things, including thinking wrong thoughts. And I was so blind to my real self that I thought I was doing very well. I measured my progress by how much I read my Bible and how often I prayed. I was quite impressed by my progress until one day a thought came into my mind which could only have come straight from Satan, and I realised then that there was nothing in me that was impressive at all. But what happened was an eye-opener to me, because I'd never before felt sin to be offensive. That was a new discovery. All my life I'd heard people talking about being convicted of sin, and for the first time I knew what they meant. This was reinforced by something that was said in the preaching at that time, 'God's law is exceeding broad, it even takes to do with our thoughts.'

Suddenly I was brought face to face with my helplessness to do anything about my condition, and the truth that everything depended on the Lord having mercy on me and saving me. I shared my concern with an elder of the church and he comforted me, telling me that it was wonderful that I was concerned for my soul, and that the Lord would save me in his own good time. A few days later Mr MacQueen got hold of me. He was infuriated by the elder's advice and he pressed on me the urgency of trusting in Christ. The elder was trying to comfort me with no comfort while the minister made me uncomfortable by forcing upon me the need to find all my comfort in Christ and to find it right away. Looking back I think I probably was a believer by then, but I can't pinpoint a day of conversion. Even in my days of silly extremes, when I set legalistic standards of behaviour for myself and others, I may have been converted, because the only comfort I got then was when I thought about Christ.

National Service over, I headed back to the Black Isle. My mind was still restless and I longed to be sure that I had been saved from my sin. As I walked down the road to the prayer meeting not long after my return home I spoke to the Lord – it would be too high-flown to call it prayer.

'Lord, I'm willing to have you,' I told him, 'but you're not willing to have me.'

On arriving at the meeting I took my seat, totally absorbed in my own thoughts.

Rev. D. A. McFarlane started to speak. 'You are here thinking that the Lord is unwilling to have you,' he said. Then his voice rose to a shout. 'It's a lie from the pit! The Lord is more willing to have you than you are to have him!'

No way could I get away from that answer, from that utterly immediate response to my desperation. But it still didn't get any further than my head. Soon afterwards it did. I was standing outside our home in the dark, feeling quite disturbed and distressed, when a verse came into my mind. 'Be not faithless but believing' (John 20:27). I went in and looked up the context. The words were said to Thomas, the believer who doubted his Lord. There and then I knew I was a believer though, like Thomas, a poor and doubting one, and it encouraged me to believe and to keep on believing. Although I felt so ashamed, that was a real help to me. It is from that evening that I knew assurance of salvation.

Sheena

When Jackie came back from the RAF I knew he had changed. But I wasn't converted then and I didn't understand what was going on. In a way I felt excluded, but that wasn't his fault. Even at that stage he seemed anxious that the rest of us should be converted. Although Jackie was always great fun, that didn't change when he became sure of his love for Christ. He was very earnest when it came to his faith. As a brother Jackie has always been caring and sensitive and he tried to keep us together and on the right road. He's not the eldest of my brothers, but he seemed to slot into our father's role, probably because he was the oldest one at home after our father died. It's only now, looking back over the years, that I can see what he did for us all.

3

O let my earnest pray'r and cry
come near before thee, Lord:
Give understanding unto me,
according to thy word.
(Psalm 119:169)

Student Days

When I was in the RAF, Rev. J. P. MacQueen introduced
me to the use of tracts and the value of Christian literature.
Occasionally I would walk through Battersea Park with
him and he always had tracts to give out as we walked.
While he didn't engage people in conversation, he did
have a heart to reach out to them. After I came out of the
RAF I felt a need to try and copy him. I used to buy
books by men like Brownlow North and post them to
people I knew a little about. Sometimes I put in a 'with
compliments' slip but mostly they went 'from a friend.' I
suppose God used Mr MacQueen's example to make me
aware of the need to reach out with the gospel. What he
did certainly lodged in my heart. But other things were
happening in my heart too. I enjoyed my job as a

draughtsman, even doing the occasional contract of my own, and it allowed me to live quite nicely and gave me comfortable relationships with the tradesmen in the district. But as time passed I became unsettled in myself, and began to seriously consider whether God was calling me into the ministry. I didn't view the prospect with any great enthusiasm as I thought that my interest in cars, motorbikes and buildings would have to be shelved if he was. What I did know was that the Lord had given me a real burden to see folk saved.

John

Among my earliest memories are Jackie working endlessly at different projects, whether it was rebuilding a car or relocating a store for the groceries or whatever. He would get the job done, however many hours it took. Sometimes his projects went badly wrong, and as brothers so unwisely do, we would say, 'We told you so.' But the amazing thing about Jackie is that he would start all over again and learn something from his mistakes. Most importantly he would complete the job, perhaps not even at the second try but it was done eventually. He is great fun and easily the wittiest in the family. That often helped to lift our spirits whether in the family, when renovating our mother's Dingwall house, or while doing Christian work such as street preaching or studies. Mam was a widow from the age of 53. The older I get, the more I realise what a daunting task she had with such a large family. We all lifted her spirit from time to time as did Jackie's humour. Her laughter and radiance remain with me.

Jackie had a big influence in my conversion. My brother had a real concern for others, within and outside the family. He kept emphasising to us our need of Christ and that the essence of true conversion is faith in Jesus. He often encouraged me to seek the Lord. Jackie was very positive about any spiritual interest I had when he could have been negative about my failures.

The Bible seemed to confirm that I should stay where I was. When, in my reading of Jeremiah, I came on the verse, 'Seekest thou great things for thyself? seek them not' (45:5), I thought I was off the hook. The ministry was to my mind 'a great thing', and God's Word seemed to be warning me against seeking that for myself. But the desire to preach the gospel wouldn't go away. It was months later that I realised the meaning of that verse. God was telling me not to seek great things in this world; wealth, status and comfort among them. There seemed nothing for it but to approach my Kirk Session with a view to being considered as a candidate. And that was a nerve-racking experience. In the course of the interview an elder asked if a verse of Scripture had been given to me to show that I should be a minister. That threw me. I had no such verse. And when I left the Session I was in a state of desperation. What was I meant to do? If God wanted me in the ministry why hadn't he given me a verse to tell me so. Was it all in my mind? Why did I yearn to preach if that wasn't what I should be doing? Later that night, with my Bible open in front of me, I wrestled with myself as I had never done before. Then my eye caught a text of the page open in front of me. 'His word was in mine heart as a burning fire shut up in my bones, and I was weary with forbearing, and I could not stay' (Jeremiah 20:9). God's Word began to calm my soul. I took that not as a call but as an accurate description of what I was like. That's how Scripture has been for me over the years – not so much a vision but a confirmation and correction.

The Kirk Session having agreed that I should go forward, my next hurdle was the presbytery at which a course of studies was given to me. Going into the ministry was no easy option. First I was to attend Skerry's College in Glasgow to do Highers, and that was to be followed by Langside College where I would do further Highers as well as study Hebrew and Greek at Glasgow University. But other things needed to be seen to as well. On leaving the RAF I had returned home to Mam's house in the Black Isle and I worked from there. I was aware, however, that she was living in an unsuitable place to be left in on her own. That made me pray that something would become available for her. A house in Dingwall came on the market. Having got the agreement of my brothers and sisters to buy it between us, I put in an offer of £10 over the asking price. And we got it. Before it was even ready for Mam to move in, that house was used for blessing. Every day at lunchtime my sister Catherine and I went to the house to do an hour's work on it. One day Catherine was very concerned about her soul. After we had spoken for a while I told her to stop her crying and go upstairs and ask the Lord to have mercy on her. She did that and I'll never forget the look of peace on her face when she came down again. Mam was soon established in her new home and seeing her settled there freed me to move to Glasgow and begin my studies.

Catherine

When Jackie told Mam he felt called to the ministry, she asked if he was sure that's what he should be doing. 'You'd better be sure,' she told him, 'you'd better be sure, Jackie.' As time passed it became clear that he was sure, and he set about preparing to go. Between us we bought a house for Mam and it needed to be renovated. Jackie and I were both in Dingwall. He was working in the office of Matheson and MacKenzie, Architects and Civil Engineers, at the time and I was in the bank. At lunchtimes we would go down to the house and do some work on it. One day I got there before Jackie. I'd been crying because I knew I was a sinner. 'You've been crying,' Jackie said, when he arrived. 'What's wrong with you?' He got out of me what the problem was. 'Take that,' he said, handing me the Bible he always carried with him, 'and go upstairs and read it prayerfully.' I went up and Jackie stayed downstairs.

I remember reading Jesus' words in John's Gospel, 'Ye now therefore have sorrow: but I will see you again, and your heart shall rejoice, and your joy no man taketh from you' (John 16:22). It was as though a whole cloud was taken from me. Everything seemed different. When I went downstairs Jackie didn't say anything, but some days later he told me that as soon as he saw my face he knew I had found peace with God.

43

Having successfully completed all the Presbytery had asked of me, I faced the next step. Entrance to the denomination's training was dependent on passing exams in Hebrew, Greek, Scripture knowledge, the *Westminster Confession of Faith* and the *Larger* and *Shorter Catechisms*. Only after that did my training in theology begin for ministry in the Free Presbyterian Church. Three serving ministers were appointed as tutors, and students spent a year with each. Theology was done under Rev. D. Maclean in Glasgow, Greek and the Confession with Rev. A. F. Mackay in Inverness, and Hebrew with Rev. M. Macsween in Oban. It was a good system, almost learning on the job. Students usually lodged with members of the tutor's congregation, studied during the week and went off preaching each weekend. Several weeks in the summer were spent on placement. It worked well apart from the fact we were totally overloaded with exams.

John
I first heard Jackie preaching at a prayer meeting in Dingwall. His stutter was prominent then, but he kept going. That is Jackie, he's determined and he'll hang in to the end. When I heard him preach for the first time, I realised that if he could do it, so could I, if God meant me to. The Lord certainly used Jackie's impediment to make me realise that although eloquence is desirable it is by no means the most important thing in a preacher. One thing that I have noticed in Jackie is his heart-warming focus on Christ from his earliest days in preaching, writing and pastoring. I think he was the first one I

ever told that I might have a call to the ministry. He immediately encouraged me to write down anything that might indicate that God was calling me. To this day I think it is remarkable how matter of fact, practical and encouraging he was in his response to me regarding my call.

We ended up being students for the ministry at the same time, although at different stages, along with Donald my third oldest brother and Calum MacInnes who was later to become a brother-in-law, and several others. It was an uphill struggle for both Jackie and me to get through the work. I often admired how he kept at it. Jackie has tremendous perseverance. That is so desirable in a minister and Jackie has been blessed with it.

John Tallach

We were not always very sensible as students. Jackie, John (his younger brother) and I took a fad at one stage for studying late. It was a bit gimmicky really. We stayed up all night to see what it was like, then tried to study all the next day too.

The night hours stints were not the only unconventional studying we did. I remember Jackie and I driving to Glasgow on one occasion through the snow. He asked me to drive and, as I did, he sat in the back seat of the Hillman Husky with Hodge's *Outlines of Theology*. Jackie asked me questions and I did my best to answer them as I drove. We tried to help each other as best we could. We enjoyed real friendship and deep fellowship too. Often I think 'Dear Jackie' and pray for him.

Studying was not always the main thing on my mind. I had met Elma Sutherland in Inverness before embarking on my studies. She had much to commend her. Even as a young woman Elma was full of good, practical common sense. She nursed in Glasgow when I was there, and it helped our relationship that she was a great friend of my two sisters Margo and Marion, with whom I shared a flat. Elma and I courted throughout my student years and planned ahead towards marriage. But Elma wasn't my only distraction. We seemed to be training for a ministry that meant preaching and pastoral work and not much else. Yet Mr MacQueen's example of using literature in outreach still both inspired me and pricked at my conscience. I had seen him use tracts, and I felt that there were many good Christian books that could be useful too. And if there was a lack of suitable books surely there were believers around who could write them.

That was my situation and state of mind when, in 1966, I went to Kames with my friend Christian Puritz to services in the church there.

'You know,' he said, 'you don't do anything other than get into a pulpit and speak to the people who are already in church. Surely you ought to be doing more than that.'

I don't always take criticism kindly, and I think my reply was probably too sharp. My instinct was to defend myself; after all I did do odds and ends of other things like buying Christian literature and distributing it, occasionally sending anonymous gifts of good books to people, and leaving tracts and leaflets in telephone boxes. But even as that went through my mind I knew

I did nothing face to face. What my friend said hit home hard. When we got back to Glasgow I talked things over with about a dozen of my friends and fellow students and invited them along to a meeting to discuss what, if anything, we could and should do. The mood of the meeting was in agreement with Christian Puritz and, as a first step, I was nominated to discuss possibilities with our tutor, Mr Maclean. He heard me out, but was probably concerned that any other activity would detract from my studies. When I went back to Mr Maclean to discuss it further, he recommended that we should take one of the elders on to the committee of our outreach group. That was done. And the elder was Alasdair Gillies, a teacher who was outstanding in his patience, love, and kindness.

Our intention was to write one or two tracts on which could be stamped the name of the church using them, and we also hoped later to offer a free Bible to anyone showing a real interest. We planned a programme of tract distribution and street preaching. We agreed to go where the crowds were with our tracts and, as we were in Glasgow, that meant being outside football grounds some Saturdays. Shortly after we got going we set up a trust, but a trust needs a name. Many suggestions were made and they were all shot down for one reason or another. Eventually, in the absence of anything clever, we called the trust after the name of the part of the city in which we had found a tiny office. It was in West Campbell Street near Blythswood Square. We became the 'Blythswood Tract Society'. And with that at the head of our notepaper, a group of us set about the serious business of reaching out to others with the good news that Jesus Christ can save sinners, that he had done it for us and he could do it for them. It was from Christian Puritz's perceptive comment that Blythswood was born. The Lord did some remarkable things in those early days, and they encouraged us to go on.

Christian Puritz

Jackie was a student for the Free Presbyterian Church ministry having a year in Glasgow with Rev. Donald Maclean as tutor, while I was there as an assistant lecturer in maths at the University of Strathclyde. We both attended St Jude's Church; and one summer, we went together to the communion in Kames (Tighnabruaich). It was on our way back in Jackie's car as I remember, just the two of us, that I raised the subject of outreach to the lost and said there was not much of that happening in the Free Presbyterian Church and that something ought to be done.

I cannot remember any more about that conversation, but it led to the formation of what became the Blythswood Tract Society. We soon got some tracts written and printed. The first one was titled 'Hear, and your soul shall live', which included an invitation to come and hear the gospel preached at St Jude's; and another that we used was 'God and Man', written by Rev. Donald MacLean. Then we began door-to-door visiting in the tenements of Glasgow, offering our tracts and invitations to hear the preaching, but finding generally a widespread lack of interest.

Jackie was full of ideas and energy. We were soon in possession of an office in Blythswood Square and we began holding open-air meetings in Sauchiehall Street. Mr Maclean was delighted with the work going on. Jackie had a great ability to get things done, and to get on well with people and motivate them to give help when needed. He focused on achieving what could be achieved, rather than speculating about it. He also had quite a sense of humour. I remember once when several members, some no longer living in Glasgow, came together to discuss Blythswood business, we had lunch at a restaurant. The starter was listed as game soup, but Jackie, after tasting it, expressed his doubt about the grand title by saying, 'I think it was done to death with an ox's tail!'

One fruitful episode in early days (1967) was when we used a tract entitled 'Mormons: Their lies exposed and their doom foretold', written by William MacLean, then Free Presbyterian minister in Gisborne, New Zealand. We distributed this to all the houses in Kent Road. (We didn't use it any more after that because I had misgivings about some inaccuracies of detail in the tract and felt that it should be revised, and we never got round to doing that.) One of the houses was that of Anne Todd and her husband and children. Anne had become concerned about God, and had been visited by Mormons, who seemed very plausible.

Anne Todd
It was in the December of 1967 that I was visited at our home by some Blythswood Tract Society

distributors who belonged to St Jude's Free Presbyterian Church. Before that a couple of Mormons came to instruct us in the Mormons' heresy, although at that time I didn't know whether it was heresy or what it was. They had been coming for several weeks before I had any contact with the young men from St Jude's. The Mormons seemed to me to be upright, good-living young men; they were very polite. But on the Saturday I was visited by Don Ross who brought a tract and across the top of the tract were the words 'Mormons are notorious liars'. I looked at this tract and I said, 'Don't you tell me that Mormons are notorious liars because I intend to be baptised by them next February.' Don said, 'Whatever you do, young lady, don't do that.'

Shortly after that another young man came up. He was Christian Puritz. He explained to me that the Mormons were not right. After listening to him I said, 'It's all very well for you to say that these people are wrong, and they come up and say you're wrong! So how do I know who's right and who's wrong?' 'Go on to your knees and ask God, and he'll tell you who's right and who's wrong,' Christian advised. I did pray to God that if the Mormons were wrong that he would show it to me, and if I was following them for any wrong reason that he would deliver me, because they were terrific flatterers and I knew that if I wanted religion I wanted it for the right reasons and not for any self-indulgence. Christian said that he would come up the next day, which was Sunday, and speak to the two young Mormons.

Christian and the Mormons discussed the rights and wrongs of each others' profession. I can't honestly say that I understood much of what they were talking about, only that suddenly they – the Mormons – seemed to imply that God was not eternal. Now I was very black, dark, and ignorant, but I knew that if God was, then God was eternal. I didn't know that God was, but I knew that if he was, then he had to be eternal and he could not be otherwise. I said, 'I can't accept that. Either God is and God is eternal, or God is not.' 'Well if you believe that,' Christian said, 'you can't believe what these people are teaching.'

That night I went to St Jude's with the children and Christian and it was a bit of a culture shock. I thought the singing was dreadful and I didn't understand much at all of what was said in the pulpit. But one thing did impress me, and that was when I came outside and I was talking with Cathy Ross and her husband Don, who is Jackie's brother, they seemed to possess something. So this did interest me. I started going round to Don and Cathy's, and Don was extremely kind and patient as he tried to instruct me and lead me to the feet of the Lord Jesus Christ. He had given me *The Westminster Confession of Faith* to read, and of course at the very first they had given me a Bible. So I was reading my Bible, and I tried to read the Confession of Faith, but it was quite heavy going.

This went on for some time until one day, as I went about my housework (I stayed at the top of a flight of stairs, in a tenement building), I was brushing the stairs when it was suddenly as if a light shone into my soul. Not literally, but mentally; a light shone into my soul and the unbelief that had plagued me for so long and driven me to distraction was completely dispelled. I believed that the Lord Jesus Christ was the Son of God. I was given faith to believe that. I believed that the Bible was the Word of God. I was given faith to believe that, and I have never lost that faith. It has been tried and I've been tempted. I've been tossed and I've been up and I've been down, but I earnestly believe that the Lord Jesus Christ is the Son of God and that he died for me and that God the Holy Spirit took of the things of Christ and revealed them to my soul.

On that day I knew that the bliss and the peace that flowed into my soul had to be of God, and I was as light as a feather the whole of the day. It was as if I was enclosed in a bubble that nobody could get through and my heart was on fire with love to God. But there was no-one I could tell. My husband and my brother-in-law were drinking and I couldn't speak to them. I couldn't speak to the family either. I felt I couldn't speak to anyone. Don Ross came to my door that evening and I was so bursting with the truth of it and so desperate to tell someone, I said as I opened the door, 'Mr. Ross, I've found my Saviour.'

Now, nearly thirty-five years later, Anne is severely disabled but she is still rejoicing in the Lord. She lives in England and is in close touch with Baptist friends of ours who care for her and with whom she has fellowship. Encouragements such as Anne Todd's conversion spurred us on and still do. God seemed to be showing us that there was a work to be done outside the pulpit, outside church doors, a work that reached out to people who would never think of darkening a church door, they wouldn't think it was for them. But there were discouragements too, and some of them came from within the church. Our efforts were not universally approved of, and for different reasons. Some thought that divinity students should stick to their books all week and their preaching on Sundays, others argued that we were 'casting our pearls before swine' and one or two doubted the orthodoxy of our behaviour.

John Tallach
I was a fellow student of Jackie's and involved in Blythswood from when I went to Glasgow the year after it was set up. We wrote our own tracts, a job we were very earnest about as we chewed them over line by line. It was a reflection of our Free Presbyterian mindset in these days that we tended to think that we did things right and nobody else did, hence we wrote our own tracts rather than using ones printed elsewhere. But the very fact that we were thinking about those outside of the church showed that to some extent our vision was changing.

I think part of the reaction we met was discomfort because of change rather than disapproval, though that is what it sometimes felt like. But there was encouragement too. Old ladies backed us financially and assured us of their prayers for the work we had started. Elders gave donations and were a great support to us. Young friends joined us in the work. But then, as now, it was hard for church folk to absorb people whose lifestyle was so different. We seemed to be associating with disreputable people from model lodging houses and met with men and women who were dirty and smelly, and who might help themselves to what was in any old lady's handbag.

Nothing prepared me for what I saw in the model lodging houses we went to. Men shuffled about, waiting for their turn on the communal cooker where they would throw together whatever they had begged or got by other means. One man made a special impression on me. He was a doctor who had blotted his copybook and no-one in his family would have anything to do with him. But he had managed to sort himself out to a certain extent, in that he was living soberly and caring for those around him. He had wider concerns too, reading the papers and keeping up with what was going on in the outside world. I came to the conclusion that perhaps the Lord was leaving him there to look after the men around him and gain a measure of contentment even in that awful situation.

In these houses, some, especially among of the older men, took me under their wings, looking out for me as a friend and keeping an eye one me rather than seeing me as a missionary. And some of the men I met there still burden my heart. There was one, he looked between 70 and 80, but was only 45. Later I realised that we had lifted potatoes together when I was a child in Ross-shire. He was a complete wreck, an alcoholic, who felt that nobody in the world cared for him. I knew his family connections and how his situation would have broken their hearts had they known what it was.

It wasn't all misery; there were plenty of light-hearted moments too. It was a strange mixture of light relief and solemnity. For example, the men would banter about the food they were eating, discussing it as though it were the best steak they could possibly have, when it was only scraps from a street bin. I'm an emotional person, and it wasn't unusual for me to cry, especially with the older men. I've always recognised this aspect of my character and I don't think it's a disadvantage, though at times it's embarrassing. Among the lean, the mean and the down-and-outs, I never met anyone then, nor have I met anyone since then, in whom I couldn't see myself. I've seen some terrible things in my life, but the truth about each one of them is that, 'There, but for God's grace, go I.'

John Tallach
We were naïve and ignorant, thinking that men from model lodging houses were ready for the culture shock of going into a church, a Free Presbyterian one at that. But they did come sometimes and often they weren't impressed a bit with the preaching. One night I was preaching a sermon which, the following day, would be constructively criticised by Mr Maclean. But I got damning criticism first when a man from the model lodging house asked Jackie why I didn't stop at 8pm when everyone was asleep anyway. I believe that Jackie bribed that man, giving him 2/6d to come to St Jude's Church that night. He was a man of means in that respect!

Marion

For the first part of our time in Glasgow, Jackie and I shared digs. Then, when our sister Margo came to the city we moved into a flat together. We got on fine. Jackie was out all day and because I was a nurse I was on shift work. Blythswood took up much of his time, as did Elma, who was Margo's best friend. Elma and I nursed together, that's why we were in Glasgow. Jackie often brought Blythswood folk back to the flat with him, and they talked for hours. Sometimes when we were in on our own he practised his sermons on me! I wasn't much involved in Blythswood though occasionally I handed out leaflets. Jackie and the others got a bit of stick for what they did, but it seemed to bounce off him and he never lost his direction and interest. He wouldn't say it, but I think he must have been hurt sometimes. I certainly was. But in view of our tradition, what these young men did was very daring. There was a hard core of thinking that Jackie and his friends were too independently minded and not subservient enough.

Calum MacInnes

I was about to begin my training for the ministry when I read the following in the Free Presbyterian Magazine, 'At a meeting held at Inverness, 3rd April, 1962, the Northern Presbytery received Mr John W. Ross, member of our Dingwall Congregation, as an irregular student studying for the ministry of the Church. A. F. Mackay, Clerk.' As I was two years ahead of Jackie (John W. Ross) in my training for the ministry, we only had that year in Glasgow together. All six of us who were students at the time were involved in the beginnings of Blythswood. We handed out tracts in the city centre and preached in Sauchiehall Street on Saturday nights as well as making visits to pubs and model lodging houses. When we asked if we could hand out tracts in one public house, the answer was that we could, providing we didn't chase all the customers away!

Jackie was Blythswood's first Chairman, he was the hands-on organiser. He and Ian Tallach spearheaded the work and the rest of us were willing hands and feet. Although we met opposition, especially to the street preaching, our tutor did write a short tract for our use. When the Northern Presbytery accepted Jackie it was as an irregular student, the irregular referring to the fact he was to undertake a modified course of studies, but the years were to prove him irregular in different and challenging ways. One Free Church minister said at the time that we were Free Presbyterian students who found an exit for their energies outside the church, the implication being that we weren't able to do so within our denomination. And he was perhaps right.

John Tallach

Jackie Ross is not an orthodox person. That's one of his strengths. There are some people who, in theory, have a commitment to mission and all sort of things, but it seems to me that they are stunted because they are controlled by what is acceptable and what will go down well in church. That's not true of Jackie. He has a profound respect for the church. He is not a troublemaker or someone who has truck with change for the sake of change. But he is completely committed to the gospel and to its extension. That's why he has the strength to diverge from the norm if that's what the interests of the gospel require. Courage is one of his hallmarks. His courage comes from commitment to the gospel. That commitment to the gospel means that he is open to the leading of the Holy Spirit, who sometimes takes us away from what is the accepted norm in the church.

I've always felt indebted to Jackie because he gave us a hefty push in the direction of making us think of those outside of the church. I didn't have the vision, and even supposing I'd had the vision I wouldn't have done on my own what we did together. Where Jackie sees opportunities and is driven on by what he feels might happen, I tend to be crippled by seeing all the negative possibilities. He supplied something that was grievously lacking and that has enriched me and, I hope, my ministry. Following his leadership I was faced with preaching outside the church, and one of the benefits of that is that you are better able to preach inside it too.

For its first few years Blythswood was a committee-run organisation but, as those who had been instrumental in setting it up scattered, running it became increasingly my responsibility. This was by default rather than design, but perhaps part of the reason was that I wasn't always very good at involving other people, being inclined to do things myself rather than taking the time to delegate.

4

That man who, bearing precious seed,
in going forth doth mourn,
He doubtless, bringing back his sheaves,
rejoicing shall return.
(Psalm 126:6)

Ministry

In 1970 two of the most significant things in my life took place. I married Elma and we set up home in Lochcarron in Wester Ross. I knew that area from school days when I had been pleased enough to leave it behind. But, towards the end of my divinity training, I was approached by both Shieldaig and Lochcarron congregations to be their minister. Nothing especially guided me to one or the other but I felt that Lochcarron was the right place even though, from a practical point of view, it was the more difficult because of historical tensions. But the need was greater there. We were welcomed warmly to Lochcarron by the congregation. Many were elderly, though there were some school-aged children. Most of the young folk were up and off after school and didn't return when they had finished their studies or training. Right from the beginning of my ministry I got the most out of the road from Lochcarron to Glasgow, as I usually drove down to the city on Blythswood business once or twice each week.

Christabel Mackay
I was in the Lochcarron congregation when Jackie came to be our minister. He and Elma had just been married a couple of months. Jackie was different from many ministers in the early seventies. Not many of them were to be seen as he was, dressed in a boiler suit and doing manual work around the church and manse. That went down well with most of the congregation, but some thought it was inappropriate. Before they had been with us very long, the Rosses encouraged us to call them by their Christian names. Such informality was a new thing then and it caused some raised eyebrows, though most of us felt that it made the minister more approachable. In those days people put ministers on a pedestal, but that didn't suit Jackie at all. He was and still is one of the villagers. I remember once in their early days here the Rosses went out visiting, leaving a chicken to cook in their new-fangled automatic oven. They were out longer than they meant to be and the chicken was burnt. Jackie made a joke of it, saying it had been cremated. Most Highland ministers would never have said such a thing. The chicken would have been quietly consigned to the bin and no-one would have known anything about it. But Jackie and Elma didn't seem to mind people laughing at their expense. The burnt

chicken was a one-off. Elma is a splendid cook and a great hostess. Their home has an ever-open door and she welcomes everyone.

Children and young people in the congregation got on well with Jackie. He's able to draw alongside them in a down-to-earth way. And he involved them in Blythswood when it started in Lochcarron. The congregation was interested in the work of Blythswood though a few thought Jackie was dividing time and not doing as much as he could in the village. I don't think that was true. You could go to him for anything at any time and he'd help you however he could. I think his work with Blythswood made the congregation more aware of what was happening in the rest of the world.

Within a short time of arriving I made some wonderful discoveries. One was that a group of ladies was committed to praying for the work of the gospel and for my ministry. There was evidence of the way in which they prayed in the later conversions of the young and not so young. One day, as I stood at the manse gate, I made another discovery that lent direction to part of my ministry. Professor Finlayson, of the Free Church of Scotland, stopped to speak to me. 'Do you know,' he asked, 'that Alexander MacColl of Lochalsh never used to complete a sermon without appealing to the older people in the congregation?' I didn't, but I learned from that. His wise words encouraged me to see an elderly congregation as an opportunity rather than a burden. One of the most amazing conversions I saw was of an elderly man. He was so angry with an old lady who spoke to him about his need for salvation that he ostracised her and refused to speak to her after that. That was a very difficult situation in a small congregation. Some time later it changed. He was converted and I had the joy of seeing them sitting at the Lord's Table together. It seems to me that the church may be neglecting opportunities to take the Gospel to older folk. People live longer now and many spend their last years in residential care. I've not come across a centre for caring for elderly people which has not welcomed those who are prepared to spend time telling the residents the good news of the Gospel. Indeed it's my experience that older people have a readiness to hear. What an opportunity that gives to bring good news to those who may have spent years going to 'broken fountains' and who long to hear about the Lord.

Bill Byres
When Jackie was about to be inducted to Lochcarron, a senior minister of the church was quoted as having said that only a madman would go there. Jackie went, and he's still there. He has tremendous stickability and that's just one example of it. He's a person of terrific commitment and drive – he doesn't spare himself at all. Jackie Ross is the last person he ever thinks about. I think grace comes through in his life and actions in a remarkable way. There's no ostentation in Jackie, just a humble dependence on the Lord. My brother-in-law is no academic, but he's a practical Christian pastor who has achieved more in his lifetime than many very gifted people. But perhaps Jackie's main

characteristic is his compassion, and that's reflected in all he does. His work with Blythswood is an expression of his compassion. In the early days, I occasionally wondered if what Jackie did was worth the effort, because he sometimes got little thanks from people in the church, but I was wrong. It has been worth all his work and all his heartbreaks too.

I wasn't long in Lochcarron before I realised that everyone had their own church connection. But when the oil rig work came to Kishorn the population increased dramatically, and the churches united to do some things together to try and reach the in-comers. For example, the ministers of the congregations went to the camp on the construction yard at Kishorn on a rota basis to take services there. One Sunday, as I was going to take the Kishorn service, a gentleman stopped me. 'What do you mean demeaning the gospel by taking it to a place like that?' he demanded. He wasn't the only one to think that we were cheapening the gospel by taking it outside a church building. But if the Lord was willing to leave all the glories of heaven to come down to earth to secure our salvation, surely we can get out of our comfortable churches and go where the people are with the message that means so much to us. I have to admit that preaching to the people at the rigs was different from what I was used to. Often in preaching I used a rhetorical question, then went on to answer it myself. I couldn't do that at Kishorn. Once, when I did, asking who would be the best person to tell you how to prepare for death, someone in the congregation shouted out the answer, 'A dead man.'

This fitted my message about Christ having died for sinners. The problem about asking questions in that context was that I got answers. I wasn't used to that.

Since my early Christian life I've recognised the value of Christian books and one of the things I did in Lochcarron was to convert a caravan into a mobile bookshop and park it in the church grounds. That led to questions being asked in the presbytery about the propriety of that. In the middle of what was a difficult discussion, one elder announced that he didn't see anything wrong with me using the ground for a caravan because a previous minister used to graze his horses there. I never did see the connection but I was grateful for his support.

The manse was quite a big house, and it wasn't long before it began to fill up with little Rosses, five of them in seven years. My childhood dream came true bit by bit. First there was the good wife, complete with her red hair. Then came the big family, Philip, Sarah, Lois, Jeremy and Jason. Even the tractor made its appearance recently, though sadly it was only briefly. A Lochcarron man was selling off his farm equipment, including a tractor, plough and other implements. I asked if he was prepared to sell me the lot. 'Make me an offer,' he invited. This was too good to miss. 'A thousand pounds?' 'Done!' The tractor had sat for some time, but it didn't sit much longer. I got it loaded up with the implements and drove it from Lochcarron to Achnasheen, twenty five miles of dream come true, before handing it over to Jeremy. He then took it to Blythswood's depot at Deephaven near Alness, to be prepared for some Eastern European project.

My ministry has been a marriage of Lochcarron and Blythswood, and sometimes that marriage has taken place in the hearts of those who have listened to me. One Sunday, many years ago now, a holiday maker arrived in church. I was preaching on Christ as King – the King who is totally in control. The man who was visiting had lost his son in a motorcycle accident and he was in a state of rebellion against God. The sermon was undoubtedly a word in season for him even though it was a plodder's effort at a sermon. Something of his previous zeal was restored. He went home, became involved again in Christian work in his community and set up a Blythswood shop in his own town.

The incentive to do anything is the possible success it may bring. But the Christian ministry is different from any other area of work because its success is in God's hands. He is sovereign, and he has so arranged things that he will have a people for himself and they will be gathered in. His Word will not return to him void. So there is certainty of success, and that success will last because it depends totally on God. I have every incentive to go out with the Gospel because I have the guarantee of success, even if I do not always have evidence of it. Mr McFarlane, my minister in Dingwall, might have been looking and for a long time not seeing the kind of success he would have liked. Yet later, from his ministry, there were four from our family, four from the Tallach family, as well as several others from his congregation in ministry, and many others were born again. He and Free Church ministers who were used in the conversion of some of our family did not, and did not need to, see all of that. Being sure of success because of the sovereignty of God, frees me from a burden and allows me to rejoice in what blessings I see.

Donald Stewart, elder, Lochcarron

I was brought up in Skye and moved to Lochcarron in 1980 to work on a Blythswood Tract Society's book van, selling books and distributing tracts door to door. That was nine years into Jackie's ministry. I'm now an elder in the APC in Lochcarron. Some of his sermons I've remembered over many years. For example, just before Alison and I were married, Jackie preached a series on marriage from Ephesians. That was very useful. His sermons are practical rather than academic, and he always applies his teaching to everyday living. We should leave church with the resolve in our minds to put into practice whatever was preached and Jackie certainly points us in that direction.

Jackie is very Christ-centred. I can't think of a single sermon of his which hasn't mentioned our need to know Christ and to be born again. You can labour a point, and maybe Jackie has done that, but there's no better point to labour. His heart and soul is in his preaching. I've especially appreciated his ministry at prayer meetings.

I think everyone in Lochcarron would agree that Jackie has a pastor's heart. He's not just a pastor to our congregation, but to anyone in need. He's so approachable that people who have no church connection will speak to him about their problems.

There's a childlikeness in Jackie's approach to things that appeals to many people. It is something to do with his positive attitude and his sense of fun. They can even be persuaded to help him dig his garden when they wouldn't dream of doing their own! Jackie speaks seriously to people about spiritual things in a way that doesn't put them off.

I've heard it said that Jackie spent too much time on Blythswood things and not enough on his ministry. I can't agree with that. He did travel frequently, and was very busy with Blythswood matters, but his first priority was the congregation he was pastor of. It was very seldom that he was not in his pulpit on the Lord's Day and he was always available to anyone in the congregation. We are highly privileged to have such a pastor and I feel especially honoured to be his congregational elder and to be serving with him and Mr Jan van Woerden.

Levente Horvath, Hungarian Reformed Church Minister
I spent almost one and a half years in Lochcarron, while studying in Scotland. During that time my wife and I were once very distressed, but we had nobody to tell of our pain. I felt I could trust Mr Ross, so I phoned him. He came immediately and sat for hours until we were able to disclose our problem to him. He listened carefully without rushing to meet our need with 'light advice.' Towards the end he even thanked us for the privilege of sharing our burden with him!

That was an unusual way of sharing in our need. Both my wife and I were amazed. He could feel in depth what was going on within us. That was an exciting experience. We have been helped in many ways throughout the years, yet on that evening we were granted a true friend (Proverbs 17:17 'A friend loveth at all times, and a brother is born for adversity'). That is an enduring illustration to me of the Brother who was born to us in Bethlehem. We felt very close to the truth of the Gospel on that rainy evening and since then I am inclined to thank anyone who shares his burden with me.

When people are converted through my ministry I'm amazed that the Lord can use me, and I'm even more amazed that he does. But it is all of grace. There's nothing in me that can reach the soul of a single sinner, and there's nothing in me to attract anyone to seek the Lord. Yet he has used my ministry and I'm humbly grateful for that.

Arjen van Kralingen, Ridderkerk, Netherlands
In 1981 three Dutch students, myself and two others, visited Lochcarron to work with the Blythswood Tract Society after we read a call for help from the Rev. C. Harinck, then minister in Dordrecht. Together with others we packed 24,000 Bibles for Ghana and Nigeria in six weeks.

Sunday 9th July 1981 was our first Free Presbyterian service. In the morning we heard Jackie preach on Revelation 3:19: 'As many as I love, I rebuke and chasten: be zealous therefore, and repent.' In the evening he spoke on v. 20: 'Behold, I stand at the door, and knock: if any man hear my voice, and open the door, I will come in to him, and will sup with him, and he with me.' He preached on Christ's gracious invitations. We open the door of our hearts to everything - ought we not to open for Christ? If we were invited to the Royal Wedding (of Charles and Diana, which was to be on 29th July 1981), would we refuse? It was as if I heard Christ's friendly voice for the first time – and I think in a way I did hear him for the first time. Christ was brought near in the preaching of the everlasting Gospel of salvation in the plainest terms.

Jackie's preaching of the 'free offer' was simple, straightforward, and above all Christ-centered. A Scottish minister's son once said to me: 'My father would walk ten miles in his pyjamas to hear Jackie Ross preach the free offer of the gospel.' He never missed an opportunity to confront the unconverted. On Sunday 26th July 1981 there were communion services in Plockton. After the services Jackie concluded the day with a short address, asking the many hearers who stayed away from the Lord's table: 'Why do you believe in God and not in his Son?' Even when Edward Ross (his brother) was inducted as an elder, Jackie spoke to his brother, then to his congregation: to those who were converted, and to those who were unconverted.

It's a great blessing to be allowed to preach the Gospel, to spread the Word. Having said that, there have been things that have been a burden to me. For the first twenty years of my ministry I seemed to live in state of constant skirmish with the presbytery over a variety of issues, mostly to do with my Blythswood activities. Others were of a deeper nature, especially regarding Bible versions. The Free Presbyterian Church uses the Authorised Version of the Bible, and that is the version I use, am most comfortable with and know best. It will always be the version I find easiest to quote. But although I'm an ordinary man I'm not an average man in the sense that I've had the A.V. in my life since I was born. Its language is not strange to me. The average man and woman today does not understand English written in the seventeenth century. Because of that I have often encouraged the use of other translations in the course of my literature work, and I have never felt a need to apologise for doing so, though I accept it was a cause of distress to some of my brother ministers. That is a source of great sadness to me, but I did what I thought to be right in an effort to spread the Gospel.

John

Jackie knows his own mind and in an argument he can get right to the central issue. You might feel he is ruthless if you are head to head with him. I remember Synod meetings over the years when he stood up, and although he did not have the flow of words some had, he'd get his point over and he would not sit down until it was said. I have often wished that I had more of that quality. He's shrewd too, in that he can weigh up situations very well, though like us all he can misjudge people. Although Jackie can be ruthless in an argument, there is an extremely compassionate and forgiving side to him. I've been left breathless on occasions when he was able to turn the other cheek and to help people who had gone out of their way to be nasty to him.

I'm blessed to have so many brothers and sisters. Each one adds a special and precious dimension to the family. Of us all, it has often struck me that

Jackie more than any of us would say he was a sinner saved by grace. I believe that as a family we all are, and would all say it and mean it, but I often felt that Jackie had the deepest grasp of this. However that's just the way I see it. God alone knows the measure of a person.

Jan van Woerden, elder, Plockton and Lochcarron
Behind every great man is a great woman, and Elma is certainly that. Jackie Ross would be the first to acknowledge that. However, he also knows the Saviour's injunction, 'Without me, you can do nothing.' Jackie's helpfulness to friend and foe alike are proverbial; even physical threats would not deter him from providing help when he sees the need. His motives? They are those outlined in Scripture. 'For this is thankworthy, if a man for conscience toward God endure grief, suffering wrongfully. For what glory is it, if, when ye be buffeted for your faults, ye shall take it patiently? but if, when ye do well, and suffer for it, ye take it patiently, this is acceptable with God.' (1 Peter 2:19-20)

It wasn't that my doctrinal beliefs were different from those of others in the presbytery so much as some aspects of my way of doing things. It did not go down well with my fellow ministers and elders and caused them great grief. Some of my brethren have pled with me to say sorry for offending and begged me to conform. But I felt that to say sorry for offending without repenting of the perceived wrong would be hollow and false.

Margo
If Jackie believes something he is unshakeable.
That's fine if you agree with him, and I almost always
do, but it must be uncomfortable if you don't. I
suppose what I'm saying is that there is a streak of
stubbornness in my brother. But God has been
pleased to use it over the years and much good work
has been done because he has hung on. It would
never have been done if he had listened to all the
people telling him what he should or shouldn't do.
And I'm grateful that's how Jackie is because it has
meant that he has hung on to his family despite
difficult times. We have had serious disagreements,
some that won't be resolved until eternity, but we
are still close to each other in many ways, and in no
small measure that's due to Jackie.

Lochcarron soon sucked me into its community life. I
came to see no contradiction between the ministry and
social, even local political involvement. I enjoyed
serving for a time on the Education Committee of the
then Ross and Cromarty County Council and that was
useful experience in the early stages of my ministry.
Later on I was a member of Lochcarron Community
Council for several years, acting as chairman for the
last few. As a result I was associated with the Liason
Committee which was formed to maintain
communication between Howard Doris, the company
who built an oil platform in Kishorn, and the
Community Council. These were challenging meetings
when local principles and values were put at risk by the
enormous influx of people who came to work and live
in the area. It is good to be involved with local issues

and I learned more about the people and place through that. When I began to study I had believed that a minister should carry out ministerial duties only. At the time of starting Blythswood, I had some serious thoughts about the propriety of doing so in case it would deflect me from my calling as a minister, until I saw it too as part of my calling. One of the things that clarified my thoughts was reading R. B. Kuyper's book, *The Glorious Body of Christ*, where he discusses the appropriateness of Christians engaging in activities outside the organised church. I thought the issue through then and found freedom to work through agencies and in areas other than the church. I have used Kuyper's book to review situations as they came along and found it useful. We must pray that we will be salt and light in a perishing world.

Among the readers of this book there may be some with whom over the years I have disagreed on practicalities or points of principle. I hope there are, because that will be a sign of their big-heartedness. And to them I want to express my sorrow for any barriers I have built knowingly or unknowingly, and to ask them to leave them with the Lord. What a comfort to know that God's grace transcends all our differences and that in eternity they will be totally forgotten and we will all be of one mind forever.

Probably the cause of the biggest upset in my life, and the event which caused distress to the people I hold most dear, came in 1989 when a group of us felt we had no alternative but to leave the Free Presbyterian Church over the issue of liberty of conscience and we formed the Associated Presbyterian Churches. I had attended the FP Church with my family, had felt called to the ministry while in that denomination and had expected to die while in it. But that was not to be.

Because we were already a small denomination and knew and loved people in most of its congregations, this was a painful and sad time for all of us. The first months and years were extremely difficult but, however we may differ, nothing we do or say will destroy the reality that we are one with all who trust in Christ alone. We thank and praise him for that. I have not at any time regretted the decision I made in 1989, but recognise that I probably should have taken the step sooner.

Although the split hurt, the issue that caused it was serious. Liberty of conscience is not the same as freedom of conscience which allows an individual to believe, practise and spread any religion or have no religion. Conscience must not be the sole guide as to how we live. Our consciences need to be informed and educated by God's Word. The Holy Spirit has to renew and give understanding to our consciences so that they operate in love to God and to our fellow men.

Liberty of conscience is the freedom to do what God wants me to do. It is not liberty to sin or live as I please. There is no freedom so complete as that enjoyed by one whose conscience is in subjection to God alone. We need to look to God who is the Father of all Christian believers, and get on with doing his will.

If anyone reading has been hurt by what I have done as a point of principle in 1989, or before, or since, please leave it with the Lord. In heaven all our divisions will be consigned to the past and there will be total unity in the worship of the Saviour.

5

Thy statutes, Lord, are wonderful,
my soul them keeps with care.
The entrance of thy words gives light,
makes wise who simple are.
(Psalm 119:129-130)

Reaching Out

The work of Blythswood, which had begun in Glasgow
when we were students, continued to be based there
after we left the city. That meant that twice a week I
drove down from Lochcarron to work in the office.
That was how it went on for the first seven years of my
ministry. My congregation were supportive and
understanding. I think they felt part of the work, part
of something more than the work and witness of a
small congregation in the Scottish Highlands.

By 1971, what Blythswood needed was a full-time
secretary. But how would we find one and how would
we pay one? Someone suggested I ask Miss Margaret
Linden who worshipped in the Free Presbyterian
congregation in Glasgow. I realised that although I had

worshipped there I knew little about her or her work other than that she regularly supported Blythswood. But when I discovered that she was an experienced secretary I wasted no time in asking her to consider working with us. She decided to give up the good position she held and take the job, making only one condition – that she would not receive a salary. She took early retirement and went into full-time work with us, working as to the Lord. Not only that, but her previous employers gave her some office equipment to start us off! They must have thought as highly of her as we were to do.

Miss Linden's heart was in the right place and her feet were very firmly on the ground. They needed to be. Blythswood, which had started off with a few of us handing out tracts, had grown. Tracts were still being distributed, but much else was being done as well. Our tracts offered a free Bible, and requests for Bibles landed on Miss Linden's desk daily. The aim had been that these would be dealt with as soon as they came in, but Miss Linden insisted that would only happen when there were funds enough to pay. She was determined to keep us out of debt and wouldn't allow us to order tracts before the money was there to pay for them. While I respected her position, over the years I've come to think differently on that subject, believing that sometimes we must act believing that God will provide.

When the good Samaritan came on the man who had fallen foul of bandits, he picked him up, did what he could for him and then took him to the nearest inn where he paid for his keep and care, promising to pay any excess next time he passed. He committed himself to further expenditure without necessarily knowing how much it would be. He saw a need and he did everything he could to meet it. So it may be with us – we may see a need and we commit ourselves to it without knowing the cost. Our Christian duty is so plain that we dare not ignore the need. Of couse that may, and often has, put myself and others under great pressure. On one occasion, when I saw an urgent need for help and Blythswood had no resources to meet it, I discussed the matter with the Lochcarron bank manager. 'I believe the Lord will supply me with the funds to repay the loan,' I assured him. 'Oh, come on,' he said, 'I can't put that on the sheet!' But he gave me the money, and the Lord did supply the repayments. I realise that there are people who abhor borrowing, but I find it better to borrow with the expectation of being able to repay, than to see a need and turn away from it.

Blythswood grew in quite an unexpected way, and within a short number of years Miss Linden was having to cope with letters from all over the world, some asking for Bibles and tracts, a number wanting in-depth study material, some needing help and guidance, and an increasing number requesting practical aid. When I gave my annual report as President in 1973, even I was surprised at the statistics I presented. From small beginnings, great things seemed to have crept up on us. We had started off by handing out tracts in Glasgow and at that meeting seven years later I was able to report that a third of a million tracts had been distributed worldwide. Over 3, 000 Bibles had been distributed. A number of book-vans were on the road, one of them south of the border. And Blythswood had even opened bookshops in Inverness, Skye, and Lewis. Because of the importance of literature work it was a great thrill for me to tell those assembled at that Annual General Meeting that 16,000 sales had been made in the bookshops and vans. We had never dreamed that our small tract society would be blessed to that extent. In our heads we would have known God could do wonderful things, but we had never imagined he would do them through us. That's a measure of his greatness.

The following year saw a big development - the setting up of a correspondence course to help those who were receiving Bibles from us. This took a great deal of organising and only operated because of a dedicated group of ladies who compiled, marked and administered the courses. Year after year we saw growth, and sprouted new branches of work. Before long the book-caravan we had parked in the church grounds in Lochcarron became another travelling bookshop. We acquired a wooden sectional building which had been the site office for the road engineers at Dornie. This is permanently situated in Lochcarron, nearly opposite the manse where it serves as Blythswood's office and store, and well as a bookshop.

Geraldine Maclennan

I first met the Ross family at Dingwall Free Presbyterian Church. Jackie's outgoing, friendly and attractive character was typical of the congregation. Mr McFarlane, the minister, was an elderly and gracious man and he set the tone. Jackie is a master at inveigling people into doing what he wants them to do, and that's how I came to be involved with

Blythswood. Of course, his persuasion only works because we all know that he'll not ask anyone to do anything he won't do himself. It was a case of, since he was doing so much, we would do what we could do to help.

In response to Blythswood tracts going out to Nigeria, hundreds of letters came in asking for Bibles. Jackie organised a group of us to read these letters, decide whether a Bible should be sent on its own, or with tracts or with a book. Then envelope labels addressed, we sent the lot to Lochcarron to be processed. I don't think that at the beginning we had any idea what this enterprise would become. The longer I worked with Jackie, the more I realised that he had a vision. Most people would have stopped at sending Bibles to Nigeria, but Jackie wanted to do more and that was how the correspondence course was born. Two ladies continued with the work we had done, and seven or eight of us began compiling a course.

I remember one evening Jackie and Ian Tallach arrived to give us help and advice about writing the course. They had brought with them a course which was already being used by a Christian organisation and had proved to be successful. Ian thought that the language of our course might be rather difficult for people whose first language was not English. He suggested that we should use fewer words of Latin origin and more words of Anglo Saxon origin. One of our group, who is an English scholar, pointed out that the course which they had brought had in fact used many words of Latin origin in a very effective and simple way. Our course remained unchanged. Despite this spirited response, Jackie and Ian enjoyed a cup of tea. As they gathered their papers Jackie turned to Ian and remarked, 'I told you we would have a rough time tonight!' On another occasion when an attempt was made to change part of the course without consulting the authors, a rather sharp letter was sent to Jackie. He phoned, thanked us for the letter and told us that he had pinned it to his study wall so that he could read it any time that he felt he was getting above himself! These incidents are good examples of Jackie's refusal to take himself too seriously.

The course was compiled in sections and sent off to Ian to make sure it was theologically correct. Meanwhile, letters continued to come in, many of them addressing Jackie as 'dear lovely brother', and that's how many of us still speak of him. The course was sent to the correspondents one lesson at a time. When each was returned and marked the next lesson was sent. That was the routine for several years and the number of students multiplied. Eventually it was decided to put the studies of Mark and Acts into a booklet rather than using individual lessons and a Bible was sent on completion of the course on Mark's Gospel. Eventually the correspondence course was administered from Lochcarron.

Working with Jackie has been a privilege. He has a good Christian spirit which enables him to get through difficulties, and he's met plenty of them over the years. Inevitably, because of the number of people he has worked with, there have been differences of opinion. Some people may hold a grudge against Jackie because of these differences, but I don't think he is capable of bearing a grudge at all. That's one of his best characteristics. He seems to be able to come out of a difficult situation, dust himself down, and move on. He also has a most compassionate heart, the kind of compassion that doesn't only see a need, it sets out to meet it. Where others see a barrier in the way of helping, Jackie only sees something to be overcome. I've experienced that in my own family when a Polish cousin came to Scotland as a refugee with very little English and requiring work. Jackie didn't just sympathise, he took him to Lochcarron and gave him work there for a time.

Another of Jackie's attractive characteristics is his quick wit which has helped him in many situations. There is nothing like a quick wit for deflecting annoyance. Neither is he slow to ask for what he wants! A day or two before he and Elma were to get married, Jackie phoned. Their car had broken down. Would I lend him my Mini to get them to Glasgow Airport from where they were leaving on their honeymoon? There was no way I could say 'no'. So off they went in my car and, true to his organisational skills, he arranged for it to be returned to Dingwall two or three days later.

Soon Blythswood was one of the biggest employers in Lochcarron. Sometimes salaries were not there at the right time, but staff worked on, struggling to keep up with the requests that came in. Nor did we plan ahead to send aid; it just happened that way. My thinking was that we should make a fast response and pay for it later if necessary. I believe that we should be like an army waiting to go into action. We should hit the ground running, praying that the Lord will preserve us on the way from scoundrels who abuse the system.

Kathmar Campbell
If Jackie has an idea, nothing will stand in the way of it. It is almost as though he has kind of tunnel vision. Many people are grateful to him for that though, as he has been able to do a power of good work over the years. It can, however, be a little trying at a personal level when Jackie, out of the goodness of his heart, tries to organise you. Having said that, I know without a shadow of doubt that if I phoned my brother-in-law and told him I had a problem he would do whatever he could to help.

Meanwhile, the work of Blythswood was spreading overseas. By the mid-seventies there was a bookshop in Vancouver and people in other parts of the world were showing an interest in becoming involved. While the office remained in Glasgow a great deal of work was being done from Lochcarron, and a substantial amount of income generated through the work there too. Miss Linden continued to work full-time and more to get through the work in Glasgow, nobody really understanding the efforts she put into it. She was a most dedicated and dutiful friend to Blythswood. It was therefore a real blow when she died suddenly in September 1977. We had no choice but to make major decisions. Miss Linden had worked without payment and we were hardly likely to find anyone else of her abilities who would be able to do that. The Glasgow office cost money to run, and there was my time to be considered. In the end there was almost no decision to take – the way forward seemed clear. The Glasgow office was closed and the whole operation moved to the office unit in Lochcarron. But before we had been long settled there it was obvious that our new premises were inadequate, so we had to roll up our sleeves and start clearing a site for a second building.

An amazing thing happened when we got ourselves established. You would have thought that the city of Glasgow, with a million people in it, would have provided more volunteers than we could ever have used. It didn't. But when we moved to Lochcarron, Christians came out of the woodwork on all sides and from several denominations volunteering to help. Although we had full-time staff, we needed help in the office and bookshop to process the orders that came in from all over the world. So much went out every day that we had an arrangement with the Post Office for their van to collect it. We didn't get that in Glasgow! Another advantage of Lochcarron became clear over the years that followed our move there. We were like a needle in a haystack in Glasgow and people had to go to some considerable effort to find us. But if someone found Lochcarron they found Blythswood. Visitors came from all over the UK and from many other countries too and they had no problem finding a parking space.

One person whose name cannot go unmentioned is Rev. Ian Tallach. As well as being a very close friend of mine he was a good friend of Blythswood too ... night or day. I often drove to his home in Perth in the very early morning, arriving before he was awake. On my way I'd stop to buy fresh rolls, and the first the Tallachs knew I was there was when the smell of cooked bacon reached their bedroom. Ian was more likely to be on the road late. He would come to Lochcarron to work on Blythswood business and keep at it until the job was done, even if it was half way through the night. Then he'd leave and drive down the road to Perth.

Anne Tallach

Ian and Jackie did a great deal of work together and we were very close friends. No friend could be more helpful than Jackie. He had a key to the house and made himself at home. On one occasion Ian and I were late home for the children's school lunchtime, but we need not have worried because before we got back Jackie had arrived, realised the situation, and was feeding them all with sardines on toast. Just occasionally his helpfulness went to extremes. When we were all students in Glasgow, we went in Jackie's car to the Oban communion. We were accompanied on the return journey by a car-full of friends from Edinburgh. Near Dalmally their car broke down. Jackie, helpful as ever, decided to run our stranded friends to Edinburgh leaving us to call for the AA and then wait for his return. It was November, and we ended up making a campfire to keep ourselves warm as we waited. Dalmally to Edinburgh and back is not much short of 200 miles! By the time we got to Glasgow we were too late for our morning classes, and no doubt too exhausted.

Ian was a book person, and he and I with some others decided to embark on a publishing venture. Calling the company Christian Focus Publications, we gave ourselves the address of the Inverness Blythswood bookshop and we republished two Christian classics, *The Beauties of Boston* and *A Basket of Fragments* as well as a few children's books. It was never our intention only to republish old books, but we chose two that were well respected in our theological group thinking that by so doing we would win the favour of the more serious reading public. Before long we discovered that we could not run a publishing house along with everything else we were doing and without more capital. The Mackenzie brothers, also Free Presbyterians, took the enterprise over and for a time we worked together. I thank God for the way in which CFP has developed into what was our original dream. This is undoubtedly due to God's blessing and the Christian determination of William and Carine Mackenzie.

Changes in Blythswood were not only happening in Scotland they were happening in Eastern Europe too, and the opening to be involved there came about in a marvellously simple way. We knew that Blythswood tracts went all over the world because we had requests from many countries for Bibles. So when, in 1977, a request came from Yugoslavia, it didn't stand out as monumental. At that time Yugoslavia was one of the few countries in Eastern Europe where religious beliefs were accepted as having some importance. But, when there were the beginnings of a religious revival among some young Yugoslavs, the state came out in its true colours and did its best to prevent the groups concerned meeting. News of this reached the west. Blythswood was therefore glad to support a Yugoslav who, when visiting the UK, approached us with a request for literature to distribute in his homeland and even further afield. It always amazes me that when doors open, God provides what's needed to go through them. And this happened with Eastern Europe. No sooner did it begin to open up to us than a Scots lady, who had studied Russian, made herself available to prepare Russian language material. This was an exciting development. We had been aware of the oppressive regimes in which Christians lived behind the Iron Curtain, but it seemed that the Lord was going to use us even there.

The focus of Blythswood has always been to distribute tracts, Bibles and other Christian literature. But as Eastern Europe and other areas of the world opened up to us we discovered the terrible poverty millions of people were living in, and we did what we could to help. We did not plan to become an aid agency, but if you work with people in need that's almost inevitable to some degree or other. Even in the first days of Blythswood we bought fish suppers for down-and-outs on Glasgow's streets. And we had no plans to become a big organisation, which is what happened – we just tried to meet needs as we saw them. If that meant taking truck loads of bin bags full of clothes to people wearing rags, we did that. If it meant taking medical equipment and drugs to a hospital that looked more like a slum, we did that too. Where possible we also took Bibles and tracts. One of the dangers over these exciting years was that our focus could have shifted. We could have been lured into answering only people's physical needs, and there have been times when that was a real danger. But there's no point in giving material help without spiritual help, just as there's no point in giving Bibles to people who are too hungry to think of anything but food. Since the opening up of opportunities in Eastern Europe we have walked a tightrope. Sometimes we've come off on the wrong side of it, but in the main we've kept our balance.

But before ever it became easy to send goods to Eastern Europe, we committed ourselves to sending small amounts of aid and literature. We had to find how we could best do this, and the outcome was that we decided to work with individuals and agencies on the ground there. We found people in different countries who became book agents. That relieved the pressure in Lochcarron and saved many hundreds of pounds in postage. The seventies was a decade of rapid expansion for Blythswood and where we could pass on a job to others who could do equally well or better, that's just what we did. I've always felt that if I could pass on one task I had time to do another. My willingness to pass things on and leave them to others was tested at the end of the seventies. Not long after we had Blythswood's headquarters firmly established in Lochcarron, I was approached by the Free Presbyterian congregation in Tain asking me to consider being their minister. The congregation there was active and had already known blessing but, after praying about and thinking it all through, I decided it seemed to be God's will that I stayed where I was.

In 1979 we suffered a great loss. Ian Tallach, who had been in Blythswood since the beginning, and who had devoted himself to it sacrificially, died very suddenly of a heart attack when he and I were in Heathrow Airport on our way to a meeting in Holland. He was forty two years of age. While I knew that Ian went to a far better place than this poor world, his death was a bitter blow. We had studied together. He was the theologian, the thinker, the historian. When he spoke he made me realise how important it was to spread the gospel. He had a great love for Scotland and a burning desire to tell Scots of their need for Jesus and of his love for them. In a way Ian was the brains behind the book side of Blythswood and I was the enthusiasm. You need both. Ian left a young wife, Anne, and four children, the youngest of whom was only eighteen months old. While we felt deeply for her, there was a great vacant space in my life too when he died. I'd lost a friend, colleague, supporter, advisor and worker. I'd lost a pal. I'll never forget when I went to see Anne. 'Isn't it wonderful that we had a loving parting,' she said. Even in that severe providence she found something for which to be genuinely thankful to God. Anne's comment has remained with me. Since then I've always tried to part company in a friendly and loving way, and to say 'sorry', 'thank you' and 'I love you' where appropriate. It's so important to part as friends as the opportunity to do so can be taken away so suddenly.

Ian's death inevitably meant changes in Blythswood, but the literature work went on. By 1980 there were bookshops in several Scottish towns and some south of the border. And in the same year we even started working south of the Alps. Franco Maggiotto, an Italian and a converted former Roman Catholic priest, worked at Spotorno on the Italian Riviera. He had set up Fede Viva four years earlier, with the aim of translating, publishing and distributing good Christian literature in

Italian. We were pleased to become associated with him and to help with financial backing. And we were also involved in China, through a Scottish couple, Drs Cameron and Ishbel Tallach, whom we supported in a small way. Our connection with both groups still continues.

When we first worked in Eastern Europe, the Iron Curtain was an almost impenetrable barrier and we had to be very careful not to cause trouble for our Christian brothers and sisters. Visiting people in their homes was difficult and done cautiously, unless there was an 'occasion' to justify being there. Birthdays, which most of us like to forget, came in useful then. The people I met kept taking me by surprise. I remember meeting a pastor who had just been released from prison, having been incarcerated for some time because of his Christian faith. He had suffered dreadful atrocities. When he spoke of his persecutors he did so in a loving and forgiving way. Instead of being consumed by bitterness he was filled with compassion for their souls. I don't know what I'd expected, but that took me aback.

Another person we met was involved in Christian witness in his university and he suffered a great deal because of that. The authorities did everything they could to knock the missionary zeal out of him, completely unsuccessfully. And he's still beavering away. This friend ministers in a denomination which is not evangelical and he has opposition from within it. But his experiences in the past have prepared him for the present. Having undergone persecution from communists he is better able to undergo persecution now. It makes me sad to think of him and what he is going through, but we are told in God's Word that we will have persecutions and he doesn't expect anything else. We've had it so easy in this country that we don't value our faith or our opportunities. God help us.

Blythswood was changing and a time came when we had to decide exactly what we were and what we were doing. We could see that the aid side of the Society would grow but we were concerned that we wouldn't lose sight of our original aims. In 1987 we defined our aims and published them in the newsletter.

Blythswood has the following aims:

1 To give Bibles and Christian literature where possible to anyone who makes a request.
2 To encourage the study of God's Word by correspondence courses.
3 To urge others to become involved in the spreading of the gospel by the use of Christian literature.
4 To support Christian outreach by making grants of Bibles and Christian literature.
5 To support financially Christian workers in Italy and China.
6 To gather and supply clothing and other materials for the use of charitable agencies and missions at home and abroad.
7 And in any other way according to the doctrinal basis of Blythswood.

As the eighties drew to a close and doors opened into Eastern Europe these priorities as stated began to be challenged by events, and over the twelve years and more since then we have sometimes been diverted from our focus on the distribution of Christian literature. But that story comes later.

6

Except the Lord do build the house,
the builders lose their pain:
Except the Lord the city keep,
the watchmen watch in vain.
(Psalm 127:1)

Manse Life

The Lochcarron manse was a busy place, and both Elma and I had our hands full. The combination of living in a manse, having a big family and running Blythswood from Lochcarron could be hectic. But there were times when I was busier than I should have allowed myself to be, times when I didn't spend enough time with Elma and the children. Without Elma I couldn't have done half of what I did. She has supported me in prayer, in a thousand practical ways, and made up for many of my deficiencies as a father. I thank God for her every day.

I think ours was a happy home. Of course, being a manse, the children were conscious of the serious side of life, and that's how it should be. And because of Blythswood they were aware from childhood that we live in a needy world. I'm glad they were. But our home was not a forbidding place, whatever some people think a manse is like, because there was a constant succession of the children's friends in and out all the time. Being in the Christian ministry may have connotations to adults, but it certainly didn't seem to stop many of Lochcarron's young folk from feeling at home in the manse. Our visitors weren't only children. We had extra people living with us – some for a few nights, others for a few weeks.

Kathmar Campbell

Elma and I were very close sisters though I am five years older than her. I married George and we had our family when we were quite young. Elma spent a lot of time with us when the children were little. She loved children. Even as a little girl she was motherly, playing with her dolls and dressing kittens up in baby clothes then pushing them around in her doll's pram. Elma was not only a sister she was a friend, especially when one of our children was born with a health problem. My sister was a great support to me then. We got to know Jackie when he was a student for a year in our home town of Inverness. Although Jackie and Elma moved to Lochcarron soon after they were married, we still saw them often, even after Philip was born. After that Elma's visits were less frequent because she soon had her hands full with five small children.

We never lost touch, far from it, but we did not see each other so often because we were all very busy.

Alison Stewart

After I finished university and returned from teaching abroad, I knew I wanted to work with Blythswood. So I asked if I could spend some time as a volunteer while I worked out what God wanted me to do with my life. I ended up staying with the Rosses for about a year and I can only describe that as an oasis of care. Although there were five children it didn't seem like that because they were so well organised. Everything was done to a set routine. The children knew what they had to do and did it. Elma didn't have to keep reminding them what their duties on the rota were, they organised themselves. And even though the eldest was still in primary school then they managed to swop round jobs between themselves to suit what each wanted to do. It was impressive.

I felt cared for when I stayed at the manse, as though I was part of the family. The place was always so busy, but when problems relating to Blythswood arose, Jackie and Elma took time to discuss them rather than let issues build up. They did that with the children too. I suppose that saves time in the long run and they were expert at pushing as much as possible into every hour. When I was with the Rosses I felt we were in the centre of the universe. Phone calls came from all round the world, twenty four hours a day, and the talk was about everything and everywhere. The phone seemed to dominate the house sometimes, but it didn't matter what time of day or night it was, or how inconvenient, Jackie was always so pleasant when he answered it. That was the kind of atmosphere the children grew up in, and I'm sure it made them outward looking and able to cope with problems, having seen how things were dealt with at home.

Previous to being in Lochcarron I put ministers on a pedestal and I didn't relate to them as people. But Jackie is a real person and he makes people feel he cares for them. I know that was true for me. There was a poster in the little Blythswood office I used with these words on it. 'Love is patient, love is kind. It does not envy, it is not rude, it is not self-seeking, it is not easily angered, it keeps no record of wrongs. Love does not delight in evil but rejoices with the truth. It always protects, always trusts, always hopes, always perseveres. Love never fails (1 Corinthians 13:4-8). Anger was something that troubled me and I thought it should always be expressed. Because of that I scored out the words, 'is not easily angered'. Jackie noticed what I'd done and restored the correct wording of the text. It meant a great deal to me, that Jackie noticed what I was feeling and what was troubling me, and took time to address it.

Family worship was part of family life. We had nursery school chairs and the children sat in a row for worship. Like most Free Presbyterian homes, we had a reading, sang a psalm and finished with prayer. We repeated each psalm over several days until the children knew it. The psalms are the only songs we use in church worship and that's what we used at home too. Although they were written centuries ago, they cover every aspect of Christian life and are a great heritage. Some people argue that because the psalms were written before the coming of the Lord they don't allow for the full expression of Christian worship. I would argue that they don't know the Book of Psalms well enough.

Cornel Iova, Pastor, Emmanual Baptist Church, Oradea
One of the things that really impressed me about Jackie was that he knew how to be a pastor to his own family. I remember those nights when all of the children were at home in Lochcarron and we all took the Bible, reading a few verses each, then singing psalms. I was accepted as part of the family too as he led us in worship and adoration of our Lord. I felt encouraged and blessed.

Jason
We had family worship morning and evening. As a child I didn't particularly like or dislike it as it was all we'd ever known. It never occurred to me to be embarrassed if friends were there when we were at worship. When I was older it began to mean more to me and now I realise it was a very important part of our family life.

Jan van Woerden
Jackie had the privilege of growing up in a closely knit Christian family. Rev. Malcolm Lamont, Free Church minister in the Black Isle at that time, lived close to their house. Mr. Lamont told me that he often stood outside the manse, enjoying the beautiful psalm-singing when the Rosses had their

family worship. Jackie's and Elma's children grew up with the same Christian privileges.

Elma

Though we had worship with the children each morning and evening, the mornings could be rushed with five of them dashing around to get everything ready in time for the school bus. Sundays were kept special. Even when they were small, all five children went to church with us. It frightens me when I see parents taking risks with their children in things like church attendance and allowing them to opt out on a whim. I liked to think of having the same commitment to taking the children to church as I had to sending them to school. While a habit of going to church will never save anyone, it will keep them where the Lord often works, and it also provides them with a support network wherever they are.

The children knew that we expected them to listen in church, and although we asked them about it when we got home I don't think it was an ordeal for them. Of course they could not understand everything in the preaching but we were often surprised by how much they did remember. Being big enough to take 'church notes' was a milestone and when we were moving house I came across a few of those notebooks. In one, the writing looks like that of a seven or eight year old. The spelling of some of the biblical terms is amusing but it was heart-warming to read the content about the second coming of the Lord Jesus Christ. Committing something to writing often implants it into our minds and I thank God that he made the seed grow which was planted and watered in their hearts by preachers of the gospel. There had to be the odd gentle nip or flick on the thigh when the note-taking degenerated into drawing lorries or exchanging notes. They too were interesting to look at afterwards.

Another significant event was being big enough to start going to the evening as well as the morning service. Our service begins at 6pm so they were able to do this as soon as they started going to school. The special appeal was that this meant sitting with other people in the congregation because I had to stay at home with whoever was still too young to go. Some of those ladies had furry coats to nestle into and, better still, they had pockets full of sweeties. What the children may not have appreciated at the time is that these people loved them and prayed for them. Ministers' families are often labelled 'children of the manse' and this is seen by them as a disadvantage. Surely, instead, it is a privilege when it includes being taken into the hearts of praying people.

Before we were married, when Elma and I discussed having children, we agreed that we'd rather not have children than have any who would not be born again. Our children were prayed for before they were even conceived. We committed them to the Lord at that stage, knowing that even then he knew them. When our five were growing up I used to think that the parents of young folk who were converted must be good. But when our own children became sure that they knew the Lord as their Saviour I realised that it was all of God's grace, not anything we did at all. Seeing Philip, Sarah, Lois, Jeremy and Jason come to faith, marry believing partners, and establish Christian homes has given me the greatest thrill.

Elma

There were many young folk back and fore volunteering and working in the Blythswood office, and our kids had a great time with them. A lady, Cathie Mackenzie, who is still in the congregation was like a second mother to them and very helpful to me. For several years we also did some short-term fostering of children. Because we already had five of our own, one or two extra didn't seem to make that much difference. We fostered eleven children, sometimes more than one at a time. Two sisters, who were fostered separately for the rest of the year, spent two summers together with us. This was the only time in the year that they had the opportunity of living in the same house. Some children came for a short time to tide them over a family crisis, like the two-year-old whose mum was in hospital. He was utterly miserable and nothing would comfort him. When I changed him and discovered sores on his bottom from unchanged nappies, I realised why he had been inconsolable. Jackie was very good with our foster children, especially with two older children who came to us in a traumatised state. Their mother had just died and they needed cared for during their bereavement. That was a tough time for our children too, because these children were older, and, coming from Merseyside, they had a very different lifestyle.

Part of our motivation in fostering was to let these children know about the love of the Lord Jesus Christ and about the hope and security that he gives. For some of them the future was bleak. We longed for them to know Jesus who would never leave them nor forsake them if they put their trust in him. Since social workers recognised that our own family was secure, I suppose they felt comfortable in entrusting vulnerable children to us. All our foster children came to church with us without protest, and they were included and took part in our family worship, each morning and evening. Although we only had children for short periods of time, we knew God could use even that. Maybe now, years after children were with us, some of them remember what they learned and experienced. That's our prayer anyway. We tried to make our home and ourselves available to them. Since our home was a Christian one, any Christian influence had to come from how we lived each day.

Jackie was often away but the rest of the time he worked from home and was more present in our lives than many fathers who go out to work five days a week. Life was exciting for all of us with an unpredictable variety of things to do and places to go with him when he was based at home. He had an uncanny ability to read and work with the children all around him. He seemed oblivious to the noise, even dozing in the chair with them clambering over him like ants. This was risky because if his mouth did happen to drop open, Lois had a good aim with

Smarties! The study door was locked when he needed peace but it didn't take much tapping at the door and of 'Dad, can I come in? Please can I come in?' for him to relent. When he was away he was in frequent touch by phone. We always knew where he was and how to contact him and that he would get himself to us as quickly as possible if the need arose. Our children liked him to tell them a story out of his head. This usually included something about Granny Ross and one of their aunties or uncles when they were young. Every few sentences he would say, 'Now I have to turn the page in my head', and he would give a sudden jerk of his head from left to right. If he forgot to do this the child on his knee would remind him!

Before the caravan and the bookshop arrived to house Blythswood's activities, the work was done from the study. A wonderful friend, Mrs Macleod, worked with Jackie as secretary. When they needed to get on with work together, the children knew that he wasn't available. At other times they would creep in and Mrs Macleod would invite them up on to her knee to watch her typing. She too was good at storytelling.

I suppose at times the manse seemed like a madhouse. There was always so much happening, and so many folk around. Jackie's involvement with Blythswood meant that people were always coming and going, many of them staying with us for a time. Donald Stewart, who is now our elder, worked with Blythswood and lived in a caravan at the bookshop for more than a year. We woke him every morning with tea and toast at the caravan window! I remember him often speaking to the children about Jesus in such a comfortable and natural way. These were winsome conversations which I sometimes overheard or learned about from the children. That's a precious memory. The constant activity must have seemed odd to some people. Everything was done with a purpose. For example, we seldom went for a run just to go for a run. It was always to go somewhere. The one real intrusion was the telephone. We had three lines and all three might ring at once, and during the Romanian crisis that could be in the day or night.

Sheena

When we went up to Lochcarron we were always made welcome. Elma was so kind and just the right person for Jackie. And the children were a real mix of their dad and mum, so there was plenty of wit between them and a great deal of fun. I've never been in a busier house. Phones were always ringing and people coming and going and staying too. I don't know how she did it, but Elma took it all in her stride. If I think back to our visits there, the two memories that come to mind are of the phone ringing and the family laughing.

Jason

Communions were probably the busiest time of year in the house, especially before 1989 when there was a split in the church. There was always a minister or two staying with us at communions. We were expected to behave, but we didn't always. At meal times this sometimes resulted in Dad squeezing our legs under the table. If we were particularly unruly, Dad would tell us to speak to him later about our behaviour. But if we did that, he'd tell us we were good to remind him and send us on our way. If we didn't remind him, he'd forget all about it.

Dad is also very impulsive. Once when he visited an old lady in the village, he felt so sorry for her being alone in her own home all through the winter that he invited her to come and stay with us until springtime. He knew he didn't need to ask Mum first because she always welcomed everyone, even for the whole winter. It was good having that lady with us because we discovered a lot about what it was like to be old. I missed her when she went away. I missed most of the people who stayed with us when they left, but it was nice to have just the family occasionally.

Sarah
Family Sundays were busy. We went to church morning and evening. The evening service was followed by a Bible study in the manse and two Sundays each month there was also an afternoon service in Kishorn. In between times we were encouraged to read Christian books and often enjoyed singing psalms and hymns together. My memories of Sundays are happy ones.

7

The children of they servants shall
continually endure;
And in thy sight, O Lord, their seed
shall be establish'd sure.
(Psalm 102:28)

Dad

Philip

Whatever our childhood was, at least it was not
tedious. It was normal for us to have people staying
with us, especially to do with Blythswood. People
were with us most of the time. Gregory Campbell,
from Northern Ireland, drove a Blythswood book-
van before he became an MP. Donald Stewart came
from Skye wearing a duffle coat. My father said he
looked like Paddington Bear. A succession of noisy
Dutchmen came from Holland. After he drove
them from Glasgow to Lochcarron they called my
father, 'the Flying Gospel.' Even if no-one was
staying with us, someone was always on the
telephone. My father would take calls at any time.
That could be trying.

We were often travelling and at least one of us would get travelsick. In June and October we had a round of Communion Seasons: Applecross, Sheildaig, and then Lochcarron. That meant going to twenty five church services in three weeks, but that did us no harm. Going to Applecross in October inevitably meant having to cross the *Bealach* in thick fog at five m.p.h. with a carload of old ladies. By the time the fog cleared we would be late and they would arrive at the church looking deathly pale. I often went with my father in a book van. Once we travelled to Keswick in an old Albion; he drove overnight while I slept on a camp bed in the back. He had to stop at every burn on the way to fill up the radiator. In those days Blythswood vehicles were notoriously unreliable.

Our entertainment was always interesting. My father enjoyed construction and machinery. I remember him laying sleepers for the building of the Blythswood office in Lochcarron. He also liked to make use of his H.G.V. licence to drive tracked excavators or heavy plant. We liked watching that sort of thing, especially when some operational fiasco would arise. He was always occupied, but I never wished for a nine-to-five father.

We all had to work around the house, and had tasks to do for Blythswood, even when we were young. There was no choice in things like packing newsletters or staffing the bookshop. Blythswood was part of my father's work and that meant it was our work too. If every house between Uig and Staffin had to be leafleted about a forthcoming book sale, we were expected to help him do it. Sometimes that annoyed us, but it never hurt us. He expected the same from us as he expected from himself. In a unique way he was enterprising and he was happy if we were enterprising as well – we normally have something to sell.

Like all of us, he has weaknesses as well as strengths. I often think that my father can be overly charitable in his assessment of people. It is good to be charitable, but perhaps he can be too dovish in his dealings with others. I cannot decide if he thinks people are better than they are or whether it is an outworking of our Christian belief that God chooses the weak to shame the strong. Certainly, a more hawkish person would come down on people sooner and sometimes that might be better, but to be as wise as a serpent and as gentle as a dove does not come naturally to any of us.

My father's greatest concern is to preach the gospel. In his congregation there were several people who had attended for many years but who had never come to the Lord's Table. He was concerned for them because they were old, yet not ready to die. Again and again he urged them to believe the gospel. Although I was a child at the time, I remember seeing some of the old people deeply moved by those sermons, not because they were genuine unbelievers, but because they loved Christ. Then there were others who were hard and refused to believe. Preaching to them seemed hopeless, but with only a year or two to spare some of them were changed.

Sarah

Ever since I was small I was aware Dad was concerned for my salvation. That wasn't just because he talked about it often, which he did, but the whole atmosphere of our home brought it out. Family worship, for example, wasn't just a case of going through the formalities. We were questioned on the Scripture reading to make sure we understood it and to encourage us to apply it to ourselves, even when we were children. We were never in any doubts that the Bible was a living book. Although Mum and Dad never forced us, we all knew that what they wanted more than anything else was for us to believe that book. When I did realise I was born again I didn't tell my parents at first. I was afraid they wouldn't see enough evidence in my life to believe me. Dad did regularly challenge me and for a while I tried to avoid giving him any chance of asking me if I trusted in Christ. I was afraid to acknowledge the fact yet did not want to lie to him. His persistence in asking me though was probably an indication that he did know already. I realised this when he told me in a letter he sent from Canada that he thought I was 'already saying "Yes" to Jesus in my heart.' He's probably quite perceptive in these things.

As children we had our disagreements but I don't ever remember arguing with Dad or Mum. We knew that wasn't right. It's only in recent years that I've come to realise what a privilege we had to grow up in a secure home with parents who got on well together. Family discipline wasn't harsh. There were plenty constraints but they were usually explained in a way that made it easier for us to accept them. Some people may imagine a Christian home to be oppressive but our home did not feel that way at all. Dad involved us in his work, be it opening letters, packing Bibles or sealing envelopes and often this would be turned into a game of some sort so that what we started doing reluctantly we would end up enjoying.

Tidiness is not Dad's strongest point but when he sees the need to tidy it has to be done there and then. If Mum was away for the day and Dad was looking after us a blitz would take place just before she was due to arrive home. Suddenly it would be everyone up and tidying, no matter what we were doing at the time. He's very focused. If tidying was to be done, then everybody was to be doing it. Dad's kind of focus can be exasperating if you are focused on something else. There have been many times when we were all doing our own thing and Dad decided something had to be done immediately. We had to drop everything and do it.

I think Dad and Mum enjoyed being busy. Even their relaxations fulfilled needs. Dad loved mending things, and they needed to be mended. Mum enjoyed sewing, and we needed clothes. My parents seldom sat in front of the television to relax. Because the manse was quite a big house, our friends thought we must be rich. We weren't. There was always enough, and I suppose that makes us rich in a world where so many people were starving, but I think we lived a frugal life.

Mum and Dad are quite different people. Dad acts on impulse and Mum is more cautious. I remember once there was a man came to the area, claiming to be an evangelist. Dad did lots for him but Mum was wary. She warned Dad not to give him money, to keep his help to kind rather than cash. I'm sure Dad may have thought Mum was worried unnecessarily. She wasn't. The man turned out to be on the run from the police. That's typical of the way my parents have worked together over the years. Dad can't not help people if they seem to be in need. I'm sure Mum's caution has balanced out Dad's impulsiveness many times.

There are some areas in which he is slow: e.g. he is slow to defend himself. Because Dad has had a public ministry he has sometimes been criticised. When I've heard people be nasty about him I've wished he would retaliate, but he has put me to shame by treating them as nicely as ever. He can quietly persevere with what he thinks is right, without being angered by how he is being treated. What strikes me more than anything else is his ability to forgive and not to bear grudges.

Although it has occasionally been misguided, I admire Dad's desire to help people. It's not just a desire he has. When a problem seems so great that many people would not help or would give up quickly, Dad persists until he finds a way of helping. I think this gift has benefited Dad in his ministry.

Lois

For Dad, caring for people is not an option; it's an imperative. But that's not always easy to live with because it meant that if something needed done, it needed to be done now. For example, Mum might have had a day planned when Dad heard someone needed something from Inverness - that's over sixty miles from Lochcarron. Dad would be in the car and off before his brain had caught up with what he was doing. Sometimes the first Mum knew he was away was when he phoned from his mobile in the car! But if, when he was on the way to Inverness he saw a driver beside a broken-down car, his focus would change direction again and that person would be the one needing help. And even if he was running late and he saw something fall off the back of a lorry in front of him, he'd pick it up and chase the lorry for miles to return it. Perhaps that tendency to think quickly and move quickly has helped him to do so much over the years.

It was my parents' compassion for us as sinners that made our home life what it was. There was never a question of us being just children and these things being left till later. Dad was always reminding us that we had to trust in Christ and put our faith in him. Those were his words, over and over again. He was very earnest about our salvation. He could be emotional in the pulpit too when he pled with people to put their faith in Christ.

Over the years, Blythswood and our family seemed to be part of each other. I don't think I resented what Dad expected of us, partly because he didn't ask us to do things he wouldn't do himself. If a lorry needed loaded with black bags of clothes, he was there with us throwing them on.

Part of Dad's way with people is that he does what they're doing. He's quite comfortable sweeping the floor in a charity shop, or tinkering in a tractor engine at Deephaven. Because he's prepared to do insignificant things, other people are prepared to do them too. Dad doesn't do things like that as an act of humility, he does them because they are there to be done. With Dad it is a case of, 'That needs to be done, and if you can't do it, and we can't do it, then I'll do it myself.'

Now that I'm married and a mother, I have a different view of the way I was brought up. When we were all together at home, things were just as they were and we took it all for granted. Now I think about it and realise how fortunate we were. It sounds too good to be true, though it is, that I never once heard my parents arguing with each other. Once, when I was about eighteen, Dad and Mum were sitting at the table discussing something and I realised for the first time in my life that they were disagreeing with each other. That was a strange feeling. They weren't arguing, they were discussing and disagreeing, and I'd never noticed them do that before in all my life. I don't think that's true of many homes, but it was true of ours. Maybe it was to do with the fact that our parents always seemed to be working towards a common cause, but most of all it was because they loved the Lord and loved each other so much. They also seemed thankful for each other.

Even after we left home, our parents were still involved in our lives. Sarah and I lived together and we had a clapped-out old car. Because Dad was on the move a lot he came to see us often, and we were on the phone nearly every day – often about the car. We're still a close family. Many people think closeness is a kind of soppiness, but we're not like that. Yet we are part of each other's lives. We are in touch with each other and meet when we can. I always know where my siblings are and what's going on in their lives. That's something we've learned from home. Dad comes from a big family and, although there was division over problems in the church, they still all keep in touch and look out for each other's good.

Jeremy

Dad is a funny mixture. His head is always in the clouds but he's absolutely on top of what is going on round about him, and he was absolutely on top of where we were when we were children. He's one of life's enthusiasts and he was always trying to get us excited about the work he gave us to do, whether it was gardening, polishing cars, or packing books. Dad could always see the end result and that's what he encouraged us to do too. That's a great motivation, knowing that what you're doing is part of a bigger picture and that you're making a difference.

As a child it was exciting being with Dad. We did things other children didn't do and went places they'd never been. Sometimes, however, there was a price. Once, when we were on holiday, Dad took us to a car auction. Unfortunately he didn't check to see if he had any money with him and the six of us had a lunch of three bananas between us. That was all he could afford. The auction was fun, but being hungry was not. That would never have happened with Mum. Dad and Mum are a real example of a happy marriage, though they used to embarrass our friends by hugging each other in the kitchen and giving each other a kiss. They had an equal partnership in parenthood. In fact, punishing us often fell to Mum because Dad wasn't around some of the time. Or maybe we behaved better when he was there.

When Dad was working in his study at home he sometimes used to lock the door. This was a real pity because the lines of the pattern on his study carpet were great for using as roads for our cars. Having Dad working from home was normal for us, as it is for most ministers' children. Of course, he was away more often than some. It's only now that I'm married that I realise life was probably lonely for Mum at times, though we often had people staying with us. We enjoyed that. In fact some were so nice I remember wanting to marry them! Although there were five of us, I think we got more attention than most children from smaller families because there were so many folk around to pay heed to us.

Dad's more of a persuader than a motivator. If you are doing something yourself it is easier to persuade others to come and help. If all you have is a vision it's not so easy to motivate people to catch your vision and work on it. Working Dad's way means that people feel he's alongside them, and he has a way of making it seem that the ideas don't come from him at all, that they come from those he's working with. That's a useful gift, and Dad certainly knows how to use it. Some might call that manipulation. I don't think it is. It's more about

Jackie's parents – Edward & Marion Ross.

Don, Jackie, Neil, Edward, Marion & Sheena (left to right).

Above Lochcarron village from the other side of Lochcarron.
Right Jackie Ross 2001.

The East Church in Lochcarron where Jackie was buried.

persuading others to see needs and being with them when they realise they can make a difference, really make a difference.

One thing I would like to learn from my father is not to bear grudges. A person can hurt him, but he still treats that person in the same way afterwards. His capacity to forgive amazes me.

I work with Blythswood full-time now, though there was never any pressure for me to do so. Since taking up the work, I've realised why Dad did things his way. I often wanted to question his judgment, and I did, while most other folk just got on and did things his way. The annoying thing is that even those of us who question him have to admit that his ways work out all right in the end. I've learned from Dad, and in many ways I try to follow his example.

Jason

I have good memories of when I was a boy in Lochcarron. There was often laughter in the house. Some of the Free Presbyterian ministers were great fun. I remember one visiting minister, Fraser MacDonald, blowing a five pound note down the stairs to my brother and me. We thought it was a great game. One of the things we enjoyed was going places with Dad in the car. He drove fast which we liked, hitting the verge and sending mud spraying everywhere.

As children we sometimes worked for Blythswood. Usually we'd rather have done something else and we were pretty reluctant volunteers. We hated inserting newsletters into thousands of envelopes but loading trucks was more enjoyable, especially as some of my friends would come along and help.

My parents are well suited. Mum's common sense could sometimes put a brake on some of Dad's crazier ideas, but not always. He still brought home a few wrecks that he was sure were classic cars of the future. I could always talk to my parents about anything. Although I never felt a subject was inappropriate, I know I often asked about things at inappropriate times. I was rather good at that sort of thing! Dad is determined, perhaps even stubborn. If he gets a notion into his head it is not easy to stop him trying to achieve it. He doesn't always go about things in the simplest way but he usually get them done. For example, if he decides at ten o'clock on a wet Thursday night that the garage needs to be tidied, even though it has needed to be done for the past four and a half months, then in his mind there has never been a better time to do it. Unfortunately if you're his son or son-in-law you have to go along with it even though it seems the worst possible time. Otherwise you'll feel guilty because he'll do it all himself. He goes right for the goal whether it's a big thing or a small one. I have often felt compelled to do things I couldn't be bothered doing because I knew that if I or someone else didn't help Dad, he would persevere and try to complete them himself. This has continued throughout his illness, to the point of his doing things that were unwise, perhaps even dangerous, for someone in his condition. However, I don't recall him ever asking me to do something which he wouldn't be prepared to do himself, though not everything he wants to do is wise. When he asked me to put some more petrol on a bonfire because a bit of it wasn't going well I did what I was told. A millisecond later there was a whoosh! and I was momentarily enclosed in a ball of fire, though not at all injured.

Although Dad is no emotionalist I've seen him cry many times, especially when he is appealing to people to put their trust in Jesus. His main purpose is to spread the gospel. This is evident in his preaching as well as it being the main purpose of Blythswood. Although he knows that people desperately need to be supplied with food and clothes, he believes that their greatest need is to know that Christ suffered in order that their sins can be forgiven. Blythswood is careful to supply provision for both body and soul. For a while it seemed to be more of an aid agency than a mission and that troubled him.

Mum and Dad were always there to answer our questions. Once when our parents were out, Jeremy and I were troubled about whether or not our sins were forgiven. When they came home, Dad came to our room and talked to us and prayed with us. Mum and Dad expected us to trust in Christ and did not seem surprised when I told them that I was sure that I was believing in him. I was about ten years old at that time, and I wanted to take the bread and wine to remember Christ's death. I asked Dad, as my minister, if this would be possible but he felt I was very young and suggested I wait a little while. However, Rev Fraser Tallach was also there and he assured me that when he was my age he was also sure that he was trusting in Christ.

Dad is an ordinary man, and he would be the first to admit his faults and failings. If people look for reasons to criticise him they will find them, as they will find them in all of us. He has, however, seen needs and worked hard to try to do something about them, even though it is, as he says, just a drop in the ocean. I admire the work he has done and his perseverance, but for all that I wouldn't like to be one of his employees. Many people have been helped through the work of Blythswood, but that's not just thanks to Dad. Many others are involved, and their work often goes unnoticed.

8

O send thy light forth and thy truth;
let them be guides to me,
And bring me to thine holy hill,
ev'n where thy dwelling be.'
(Psalm 43:3)

Literature

Literature work has always been very important to me.
Away back in 1968, I put a book van on the road and
toured it round the rural north of Scotland selling from
door to door. My journeys that summer were worked
out to tie in with my preaching engagements. On my
rounds I found that many people seem to take comfort
from belonging to a denomination, instead of the lasting
comfort of trusting in the Lord Jesus Christ. I also
discovered that people who needed someone to talk to
could unburden themselves to me, a stranger. That
gave me wonderful opportunities to direct them to
Christ. These meetings were obviously God-planned,
as often the timing could not have been improved upon.

I arrived with just the right books for situations I knew nothing about.

There were some memorable meetings that summer, some of them with incomers to the Highlands who, having no local connections, received no pastoral care and who really needed it. One lady I met, whose first husband had died of cancer, remarried. Her second husband was a widower who had lost his wife to cancer. They were still going through the grieving process and desperately needed support. The lady had at one time attended Rev. John Stott's church in London and I had some of his books in the van, and also books by Dr Martyn Lloyd-Jones, whose ministry had been blessed to her in the past. She was so excited to get these books. And that is only one example of God's providence in taking the books where they were needed, and the right books at that.

Through the work of the book-van I met all kinds of people. As we talked together it was heart-warming to see people begin to think about and understand what the Christian message of salvation through Jesus Christ was about. There were others too who would come in to browse and chat, very confident in their own righteousness. 'I've never done anyone any harm' was one of the commonest expressions. It was hard trying to break through that and to explain that it's perfection that's needed to find acceptance with God. The only way to find that is in the Lord and Saviour Jesus Christ as a substitute for us. I thank God that it's the Holy Spirit who has to work there, breaking through and showing what Jesus has done for lost sinners.

What struck me as I went from community to community that summer was that I wasn't doing anything extraordinary, just plodding on day after day, but the Lord was gracious enough to use what I was doing. It seems to me that that is how much of the Lord's work is accomplished – by just doing what needs to be done, trusting he will bless and use us. I understand that the majority of Christians come to faith through ordinary contact with other believers, and that should inspire us to keep serving as Christians wherever God has placed us. Of course, seeing how the Lord used the book van whetted my appetite for literature work. Years later, when we had a Blythswood conference in Lochcarron, it transpired that every single person there had been influenced by Christian literature, some of them away back in their childhood. Right from my days with Mr MacQueen in London, when we walked through Battersea Park while he handed out tracts, I had seen the value of literature work. But my experience that summer with the book-van gave me an enthusiasm for that aspect of Christian ministry that has never left me.

Blythswood produced its own tracts and, along with others from Bible societies, they were used by Christian friends in various parts of the UK and beyond. In the early days of Blythswood we gave out tracts on a door-to-door basis, our principle being that everywhere we visited a piece of literature should be left. Sometimes we'd be given half a crown and that paid for the next few tracts, but that was rare. Over the first few years in Lochcarron the work grew and the people there became involved and supportive in their prayers. They liked to hear of occasions where God had blessed the work for which they were praying. So often as churches or individuals we ask people to pray for a situation, then when the Lord answers their prayers we don't go back to tell them about it.

Frank Rennie
In October 1975, local government re-organisation meant I had to move from Glasgow to Lochgilphead in Argyll. As the family was not able to move right away, I lived in lodgings near Lochgilphead from Monday to Friday and went home at weekends. I wondered what the Lord wanted me to do in my new situation and I wrote to Blythswood Tract Society asking for some tracts so that I might undertake door-to-door visitation in the area. Jackie Ross responded with a good supply of leaflets and some words of encouragement. A couple of years after that brief contact with the Society, Jackie contacted me to say that he proposed opening Christian bookshops throughout Scotland, and asking if I would be interested in assisting with the project. Having a very firm belief in the power of the written word, I was enthusiastic, and when a shop in Lochgilphead's front street became vacant I got in touch with him. I was invited up to Lochcarron.

Taking a week off work, I took my wife Betty and our two-year-old son for a week in a caravan in Lochcarron. Betty clearly remembers a conversation that took place in the garden of Jackie's manse. She deduced that he had been investigating our credentials prior to our arrival, and that on meeting us he came to the conclusion that he had wrongly judged, in particular, my wife's motivation in wanting to run a bookshop. And she well remembers him asking forgiveness for his misjudgment. He was so concerned that his thinking had perhaps been ungodly.

The shop was purchased and opened with Betty (and son!) serving. Local people did not respond with much practical support. Even the Christians expressed amazement that we should think of opening a Christian bookshop. However, visitors to the town were just as amazed - and delighted. They came from all over the UK, the Netherlands and elsewhere, some only knowing of Lochgilphead because of the shop! Jackie's vision had far-reaching effects, though perhaps not quite in the way he had hoped.

Our stock was controlled from Lochcarron, and very little personal contact was possible though Jackie was always just a phone-call away. When he did visit it was as though a hurricane hit the place because he was always trying to fit in to the space of two hours what other people would do in eight. Jackie was unfailingly encouraging, even when sales were pathetically low. When we proposed moving to other premises so that Betty could be at home more and still attend to the shop, he was most sympathetic and helpful. From our point of view Jackie's best attribute was his overall vision of the wider scene, which is like a breath of fresh air to the likes of us. His worst trait was to bowl us over with his enthusiasm and leave us feeling ashamed of how little we were accomplishing.

Other shops were opened in Oban, then Campbeltown, and the Lochgilphead shop was used as the contact point. On one occasion Jackie and others came to do a whistle-stop tour of the shops. Jackie, who has a problem with a heavy right foot as soon as he sits in a car, went like a whirlwind, so much so that on our return I couldn't face the meal Betty had prepared for us. Jackie and company were returning to Lochcarron that same day and I waved them goodbye with a profound sign of relief that I wasn't travelling with them!

Geraldine Maclennan

I had been involved in Blythswood's correspondence course for some time when I had an invitation from Jackie to lunch with him in a Dingwall hotel. In my ignorance I thought I was going for a pleasant lunch, probably as a 'thank you' for organising the course. Two others arrived with Jackie, and the meal had hardly begun when the subject of a bookshop was brought up. Mrs Tallach, who had started the Christian Bookshop in Dingwall some years before, was retiring and Blythswood was to take over the running of the shop. Jackie's proposition was that I might oversee a Christian Bookshop - which seemed quite reasonable to him even though I was working full-time as a teacher! I agreed and that started quite a long involvement with the shop. I went in most days after school, meeting travellers, dealing with orders and generally keeping a watching brief. Jackie popped in regularly and he was always bright and encouraging.

He is a visionary on a huge scale and you catch something of his vision through working with him. There have been many occasions when other people would have looked at Blythswood's situation and decided to limit the Society's activities. But that's not how Jackie thinks. When he sees a need he cannot ignore it, but he has to get out and do something about it. If he can pick up people along the way who will help, then so much the better.

Working with Jackie has sometimes made me feel under pressure because seeing how much he does himself it is almost impossible to refuse any request to help. On the one hand that's an encouragement to get on with the job, but on the other it sometimes made me feel I just couldn't do any more. He was always reaching out to implement some new scheme and there have been occasions when confronted with a request to help I have had to say 'no' and felt guilty as a result. This guilt feeling is a small price to pay for the privilege of working with a great man.

In 1980 we were encouraged to discover the far-reaching effects of Christian literature. A letter came from Nigeria, from the son of a man who had written to us in 1967 after being given a Blythswood tract. The man had been deeply affected by what he had read and his son was now a believer and in the ministry. That was very exciting. You can think that a tract is so insignificant and wonder what it can possibly do but we are all little links in God's great plan of things. There are many people now in Christian work whose first contact with the gospel was a Blythswood tract. We should expect that. I'm an optimist, and all who are in the Lord's service should be optimistic. Because we are working for the Lord, what we are doing is very important. We don't need hype or great campaigns or big advertising slogans to make what we do worthwhile. Just giving out one tract can lead to a young man going into the ministry.

Sheena

My brother Jackie never gives up, he keeps going at things. Before I was converted he asked me to help out in the Blythswood Bookshop in Inverness. I wasn't very happy about it because some of the children were still in primary school, but he persisted, and I agreed to do it for a fortnight. Then he persuaded me to do another fortnight, and another. Eventually I was there for fourteen years! It worried me that I was there when I wasn't sure of my own faith in Christ, and it was awkward at times too. People sometimes came in with spiritual problems and I felt I couldn't help them. On one occasion a young girl came in with a particular problem and I couldn't speak to her because there were other customers in the shop, and I didn't know what to say anyway. I decided then that I'd had enough and I told Jackie that was it. I was leaving. I can't remember how he got round me that time, but he did. But Jackie knew what he was doing. Some of the books in the shop were a real help to me and I was converted when I was nearly forty. When I told Jackie he was overjoyed.

James MacDonald

I first met Jackie in 1981 when I was a student at St Andrews University. A group of us were thinking of starting a Christian bookshop and we went up to Lochcarron to discuss the possibility. I liked what I saw and spent three weeks working as a volunteer there in September 1982. There was endless packing to be done, sending Bibles all over the place including to about twenty bookshops which were then stocked from Lochcarron. The whole enterprise ran with very few staff at the centre. It seems strange, but what struck me was the extreme piety of it. I was required to participate in public prayer continually during the day. Morning worship in the office included two prayers, then grace was said after meals as well as before meals, and as I was lodging with a Free Presbyterian lady, I was expected to take worship at home too. Having come from a situation where I had occasionally taken part in a prayer meeting to one where I was involved in public prayer several times a day, I found it quite exhausting. I was twenty at the time and a professing Christian. There was one sense in which none of this was new to me, but the all-pervasive nature of it was. It was a real Christian environment.

Some months after graduating I went to Lochcarron to work as a volunteer, and was there for seven months. Then after a short break, I went back in February 1985 and I've been with Blythswood ever since. In January 1984, answers had started to come back to the Mark and Acts booklet. Each comprised 500 questions and every single one had to be marked. Markers had been appointed but the piles of incoming envelopes were not reaching them; they were accumulating in Lochcarron. In a way this was not untypical of Jackie. He knew what stage one was: putting the course together and sending it out to those who asked for it, but not so much thought had gone into stage two, what to do when answers started coming in. My job was to service the markers and send the Bibles out on successful completion of the course. These went all over the world, but mainly to West Africa. The geographic spread remains the same today.

In the mid-eighties Blythswood went through a time of financial difficulty and a few of the bookshops closed and others were taken over by local Christians. There were often piles of literature waiting for money to come in for postage, and stacks of Bibles packed ready to go out. That's no longer the case which makes my work easier. Now I can post out as much as I like, even taking into account the shoebox literature project each year. In the year 2000 we sent out 42,000 items. Despite all the financial ups and downs we're still here, and God has used the Society in many wonderful ways.

The Mark and Acts correspondence course peaked in 1992-93, with 8,000 people completing it, and since then it has gone down, mainly due to the worsening situation in Nigeria. In 2000 we sent out fewer than 600 Bibles under Mark and Acts, but we anticipate that will increase. Most of our students are in Nigeria where there are vastly more Christians than there are here, many of them unable to afford to purchase a Bible. The shelf life of literature is considerable, even of correspondence courses. We are still getting answers to courses sent out ten years ago. My own commitment is to the West African aspect of the work, particularly Nigeria. But that's a small part of Blythswood's ministry now. The organisation has grown and changed, especially since Eastern Europe opened up in the late eighties. Literature is only a small part of it now; most of the effort goes into aid.

Over the last sixteen years I, like Jackie, have been based in Lochcarron. Sometimes I felt that he wasn't paying attention to the work I was doing, but he says that he didn't always need to be involved because he knew we would get on with the work without him. Having said that, he's a very hands-on person when he needs to be, taking on everything from building projects to clearing drains and everything in between. And when Jackie does things other people get on and do them too because he's a great motivator. One of his shortcomings is that he tends to start projects without considering how to continue them. He is wildly optimistic, unreasonably optimistic. But it has paid off, I've got to admit that.

For a few years, because of the sudden and overwhelming cry for material help in Eastern Europe, our time and effort became concentrated on aid supplies, with some literature being added. And I don't think that is going to change as long as there is evidence of that kind of need. But I do hope that now, with our much more structured management and hugely increased staffing levels, those of Blythswood's workers who care deeply about literature work will focus more on it again. In fact that's already happening. Blythswood runs successful bookshops in Stornoway, Portree, Dingwall, and Lochcarron. We now have a Christian book club (Books for Life) up and running, and recently we put a Christian book-van back on the road. That gave me real pleasure. One of my great sadnesses over the years has been the demise of the book-vans, and I have often said that I hoped to live long enough to see one back on the road. God has graciously granted me the answer to my prayer and a book-van is again working in the Highlands and Islands. Our charity shops are developing Christian Book Departments where the stock is keenly priced, making it accessible to most customers.

9

But I both poor and needy am;
come, Lord, and make no stay:
My help thou and deliverer are;
O Lord, make no delay.
(Psalm 70:5)

From Ross-shire with Love

The aid work Blythswood does in Eastern Europe is
very important but it can almost take over because
people respond to it much more freely than they would
to an appeal for money for Christian literature. It's
difficult to keep the balance right and we've strayed
from time to time. Yet we must not ignore people's
physical needs. There's no point in telling folk to be
full and clothed without giving them something to eat
and wear. God requires us to love our neighbour
unconditionally. And we should never give aid on the
condition that we can preach to people – giving should
be an act of simple compassion. In Blythswood we
give aid through churches, especially in Eastern Europe,
and we give it on the understanding that it will be

distributed unconditionally and with a readiness to share the gospel message as opportunity arises. There is a view that giving does more harm than good by making 'rice Christians,' whose only interest in the faith is in material aid. The logical conclusion of that would be that Jesus' methods were wrong. He fed 5,000 hungry people who then followed him because he had provided them with bread. Yet, within a short time he did the same thing - feeding 4,000 people in compassion for them because they were hungry. We should give people what they need when they need it.

Several years before Eastern Europe's dramatic fall of communism in the late eighties, we were able to gather and send aid to Poland and to Armenia in their time of crisis. My first visit to Romania was with my brother Don in 1987, two years before the Revolution, when it was very difficult to enter the country and to move around once inside. Yet within two-and-a-half years, Blythswood was engaged in a major aid project. Strong pleas came to us for agricultural equipment. We thought we could never provide that – it was rather a jump from bags of used clothes – but God knew better. Even before we had prayed about it we were offered a tractor and implements! We collected several tractors after that, some of which seemed at the end of their useful lives. But our volunteer workers included mechanics who overhauled them before they were sent out. Those tractors and implements are still in use.

One day I was sitting in a Romanian restaurant, eating something that seemed at a very reasonable cost to a Westerner, when a poor-looking man came in. He came over to my table begging but, before I could do anything, along came a waiter and the man was out on the street in double quick time. When I left the restaurant I found the man. He wasn't begging. He was crying. I could understand that the waiter had to take care of the restaurant's clientele and keep beggars out. But my heart was torn when I saw that man. His desperate situation had a profound effect on me. On another occasion I saw someone who was evidently in need but not begging. When I gave him a little money he burst into tears.

Giving money to people or groups instead of aid is something we have had to think through. Sometimes groups working within a country have shown that it is more effective for us to appeal for money on their behalf. They can purchase goods locally and provide immediate relief. At other times we have been asked by people in, for example, Rwanda and Romania not to send money, but to send aid in kind, because the medicine, the food or whatever was needed was not available to purchase anyway. It is often more effective to deliver goods and see to their distribution. Much depends on the recommendation of those who are working directly in the situation where the need exists. We pray for wisdom in how we give, and are often thankful for the Lord's clear providential leading, which is a fulfilling of his promise to give us wisdom when we realise our lack of it and ask him for it. That is a promise from James 1:5.

Elma

In 1988 we decided to take the children on holiday to France, but it ended up being much more adventurous than that. Because we wanted to meet the people we'd heard so much about we planned a route through France, Italy, Yugoslavia, Romania and home again. We took all sorts of goods with us that we intended leaving in Eastern Europe. Even the children's clothes were carefully selected so that they could bring back the absolute minimum and leave the rest behind. We had ten days in France, that was the holiday part of the trip, then we went to Italy where we met with Franco and Aurora Maggiotto. We had prayed for years for them and their work and it was great to meet them. Then we headed to Yugoslavia. I could hardly take in how beautiful it was. It is hard to think of the devastation of these beautiful towns and villages that has resulted from the recent wars there.

After Yugoslavia we turned north towards Romania. The children were so excited, seeing it as a big adventure. But I knew Jackie was tense as we reached the border. He wasn't the only one. The border crossing gave me the shivers. The guards were armed and the soldiers had automatic weapons. Philip opened the back of the seven-seater so that it could be searched, but a bottle of fizzy water fell out and exploded when it hit the ground. Suddenly the soldiers' guns were pointing in our direction and the car was surrounded. There was an awful moment; then one of the guards realised what had happened, nodded, and their guns came down again. They ordered the children out of the car and all except Jason did what they were told. Jason was sound asleep, and when the customs officers searched the car they shoved him aside like a sack of potatoes. We were so relieved when the search was over and we were waved through into Romania.

The hotel we stayed in that night sounded grand - Hotel Intercontinental. There was no hot water and no light bulbs in the rooms. Breakfast was much worse than we'd expected, even though we'd heard about the situation there from Jackie. We really did struggle to eat it. But meeting Jackie's contacts made up for everything because they were so pleased to see us. There were no loud welcomes though, as it wasn't safe for them to have British people in their homes. Before we left Romania four days later we had given our friends the Bibles and other gifts we'd brought from home, as well as all the clothes we wouldn't need. The car had been packed to the gunwales when we left Lochcarron and was virtually empty on the way back. In a way it was a relief to leave Romania though part of all of us remained there and still does. We'd all been involved in Blythswood's aid work before that holiday, but it made a difference after it to be able to picture the people and remember the places.

Some of the Christians we met then had no doubt that the downfall of communism was on its way. They were praying and they were certain their prayers were about to be answered, though some were surprised by the suddenness of it all. The fall of the Berlin Wall was a symbol for the world, but it was more of the same for the people who lived in Eastern Bloc countries. That kind of thing was going on all around them in ways they hoped would change their lives. We were certainly aware of differences when it did. Before the revolution border guards were awkward, suspicious and officious and you couldn't trust them. Right after the revolution they would come out and hug us, although that still did not necessarily mean you could trust them! It was quite amazing to experience the 'before and after'. But I was shocked by how unprepared we Christians were to grasp the opportunities the new openness provided. Jehovah's Witnesses and Mormons were right in there with literature they already had prepared. Believers in the former communist counties were ready, and they made the most of their opportunities.

When the revolution hit the news we took our book-vans off the road, filled them and four hired trucks with aid and drove straight out to Romania. But as soon as you divert resources in that way it's difficult to refocus them again. And as the dreadful conditions in Eastern Europe became more widely known it was hard to get excited or excite other people about distributing Christian literature . Everyone's mind was on aid. We sent out aid to Jews in Russia. They would accept it only on condition that no Christian literature was included with it. We respected that and trust that we lived the gospel. There was no way we would refuse to help people in need because they didn't want Christian literature or showed no interest in the faith.

There were others who desperately wanted Bibles and whatever other literature we could give them. When we took aid to Eastern Europe in vans with 'Lochcarron Christian Books' painted on the side, people came and asked for Bibles and books and went away crestfallen when we said we had none, that we were using the vans to deliver aid. We in the West have no conception of the hunger there was for God's Word in people who had lived under communism for many years, some of them all their lives. For the first time Christians could go and hear preaching in public and could read a Christian book without fear of being discovered and arrested. And many who had shown no interest in the faith before, maybe because they were afraid of the consequences, wanted to know what it was all about.

Each visit to Eastern Europe opened my eyes to some new aspect of the situation there. Once, as we were crossing the border into Romania, the guards questioned us closely about our load. Did we have pornographic material? Did we have guns? If we did, they didn't want us in Romania. Their's was a good country, a country without a crime problem, and they didn't want to import one from the West. Yet what we saw and heard was different. We discovered that some of the vast number of prisoners in Romania were locked up for the crime of stealing food to feed their children. But there was compassion to be found even in the prisons. We met a governor who was deeply affected by what he saw every day around him. He planned to distribute any aid we could give him to the families of his prisoners who, he freely admitted, were in desperate need. His aim was to give support to families as they visited and to send stuff out to their homes too. An Orthodox priest who was involved in that prison was not too happy with our 'interference'. He persuaded the governor to allow him a room to decorate for the prisoners to use as an Orthodox place of worship but he curtailed the work we could have done there to make the prisoners' lives more useful.

I think that one of the worst things I've ever seen was when we took aid into a country I don't want to name. Our planning went all wrong as we had two or three drops at different places and they took much longer than we'd thought. Eventually, at 2 am, we arrived at an old people's home to leave things there. The person who was responsible for the establishment had gone home leaving no care staff in the building at all. The door was barred from the outside. When someone was found to open the door for us, we offloaded the bags we had brought. The stench was indescribable and the temperature inside was bitter. It broke my heart to think of old people ending their lives there. I imagined one taking ill, or falling, and there was absolutely no way of getting help at all.

Everyone has seen pictures of Romanian orphans and street children, but for all the horror of TV film it doesn't begin to compare with the reality. The disgusting smells, the hollow lifeless eyes, the children wrapped so tightly they couldn't move, the babies so neglected that they didn't bother crying because it had never done them any good, the sheer tragedy of it cut into us when we met it face to face. And it was terrible to see those who were trying to help the children struggle to do so, with no time, no resources and not enough food for themselves. The prayer, "Give me neither poverty nor riches ... lest I steal" in Proverbs 30:8-9 took on new significance as we recognised the problems facing those working there. We wouldn't keep animals in the condition these children lived in. Having seen it we had no option but to do what we could to help. There are some situations that leave Christians with absolutely no alternative but to act – and not only Christians. No decent human being could have walked away from those children and forgotten them. I remember that as the news of the situation in Romania hit the TV screens, my bank manager said that Blythswood would have to do something about it. What an opening! I've become quite friendly with a number of bank managers in my time! And thankfully, with God's help, Blythswood was able to do something about it, and we're still at it.

What I saw on my trips affected me so that I became upset when I heard complaints in this country. Sometimes you hear someone describe a hospital in the UK as being like one in Eastern Europe. It's true we have problems here, but there's no comparison between poverty here and there, and the same is true of education, health care, orphanages, law and order – everything. We're only a few hundred miles away from Eastern Europe but we're living in another world. Romanian friends of ours were involved in a car accident when visiting Inverness and the whole family was taken to hospital and X-rayed. They were given a cup of tea there. The police who attended showed the kind of care and concern we're used to, but our friends were amazed. Police involvement in their country, even over a minor incident, is not good news. We take so much for granted here.

We saw good things too. In 1992 a couple in their eighties who had lived through the long years of communism, were converted and baptised. That was amazing. We'd taken some aid to their home village and some time later I was invited to a special outreach service. A number of people were baptised that day, but to see these two old people – it made complete and wonderful sense. They'd been bound by Communism nearly all of their lives and now they were free, gloriously free, and I could see it on their lined faces.

Finlay MacKenzie, Blythswood's Logistics Co-ordinator
I was converted in 1989. Two years later my wife and I became Blythswood volunteers after seeing a television programme about the work. Some years later I became full-time. The first time I met Jackie I went with him to Glasgow to meet people off a plane. I'd never met anyone like him. As we waited in the airport he had one phone in one hand, a credit card phone in the other, and he was speaking into both! When we heard the plane had been diverted to Edinburgh, he said, 'Good, that's us moving again.' That's Jackie. Everything is at a gallop, and when things don't work out as planned he assumes that good will come out of it. That night I drove up the road at 70 m.p.h. 'You're a good steady driver,' he told me. But what he was really saying was, 'Come on man, get a move on.'

When Jackie sees a need he goes right for it, and at speed. Take the problem of Romanian children, for example. When the truth about them came out, Jackie pulled out all the stops at Blythswood to get help. Their situation was terrible. People called the children's homes orphanages, but the children were not truly orphans. Some were there because of financial distress and some because of illness. Before the revolution a mother became a hero mother when she bore her seventh child, but there was no money to feed them so they were hidden away in so-called orphanages. In one area Jackie discovered 1,500 children in homes and three quarters of the local population didn't know they were there. The buildings were massive, four storeys high, with no heating, no lighting, and few windows. Some nurses were left with thirty babies to look after for twelve hour shifts and with absolutely no resources. When others took days off, they just locked the children inside and left them there. We charged in with help in a way we wouldn't do now. But the need was so overwhelming.

Jackie is a visionary, that's one of his great strengths and one of his great failings too. He sees a need, knows it has to be met, works out how to do it, and gets on with it or motivates other people to do it. That can be uncomfortable for those people Jackie works with because, while he wants to move forward immediately, they may want to think through a strategy first. For example, sometimes he phones me up and tells me I've got to send a load to such and such a place today and that's the first I've heard of it. Someone has told him of a need and he sees that as today's priority even though we may be fully committed. We can have a difference of opinion over things like that, but Jackie doesn't bear grudges.

He is very good in stressful situations. In Romania I was with him in a very difficult meeting, where everyone was talking at once and the atmosphere was highly charged and emotional. Jackie was being given a hard time and not once did he retaliate. He sat there and took it all, then, at the end of the night, those who had been hardest on him needed a lift home. Jackie went forty or fifty miles on Romanian roads in the opposite direction from where he was going just to give them a run home. It was 4 am before he got back for his bed.

To a degree, Jackie assumes other people will do what he's willing to do, and he sometimes forgets that not everyone is prepared to be on the road at 6 am and still going at midnight. But he's a hard man to say 'no' to. If Jackie phoned you at 2 am and asked you if it was raining, you'd get out of your bed to see rather than tell him to open his curtains. Many times my phone has gone at seven in the morning and I've wondered why it couldn't have waited another couple of hours. And when he gets an idea into his head, he doesn't let go. I've known him come with an idea, spend hours discussing it, then have to let it go because we felt we couldn't take it on. But I knew fine that he'd go back to the drawing board and present the same idea in a different way within twenty four hours. And I've got to admit that second time round his ideas are often adopted. It's a terrific privilege working with Jackie, though it's hard work.

Blythswood expanded because we did what needed to be done. Staff and volunteers entered into the work with great energy and speed. Other supporters, usually canny and taking time to think things through at least twice, gave up secure jobs and cast in their lot with Blythswood. As Eastern Europe, especially Romania, opened up to the West and the conditions there became known, we did what we could, that's all.

10

Great is the Lord, much to be prais'd;
his greatness search exceeds.
Race unto race shall praise thy works,
and show thy mighty deeds.
(Psalm 145:3-4)

The Blythswood Story

In the early days Blythswood tracts reached to far
corners of the world, and now aid does too. But
Scotland is also a needy country, and we try to do what
we can here.

*Maureen McKenna, of Open Door Trust Glasgow, which
works on the city's streets helping those in need.*
A month after the Trust was set up, we had a phone
call from Rev. Jackie Ross of Blythswood Trust, a
charity which, amongst other things, collects clothes,
furniture, medical supplies etc. from all over
Scotland, runs charity shops in this country, and
distributes aid in Eastern Europe. We had obtained
furniture from them on many occasions for families

in need. Jackie arranged to come and see us. His visit was memorable as we discussed how we might work together. Before leaving he invited us to visit Deephaven, Blythswood's centre in Ross-shire. Our visit to him there was even more memorable, beginning with a long drive through a blizzard to get there. But what a welcome! Deephaven is a vast hanger, and as Jackie showed us round he introduced us to the volunteer workers. In Deephaven, donations of every kind are processed and prepared either for sale or distribution here or for transporting overseas. We found much to inspire us.

The time came for us to brave the elements and head back to Glasgow. But Jackie wasn't finished with us. 'Could the Trust make use of an old double decker bus?' he enquired, indicating one that was sitting nearby. I laughed. 'What would we do with that?' I asked. He turned in the direction of the vehicle. 'Come and have a look.' We followed him. This was no ordinary bus. Downstairs was equipped with a cooker, fridge, sink, tables and chairs, and the back was fitted out for children's play. Upstairs was a counselling area. My heart leapt and, when I looked at my husband, I knew what he was thinking. Could we use an old double decker bus? We most certainly could. For once in my life I was speechless! 'Think of taking the bus out on the streets at night,' Hugh, my husband, said. 'We could prepare the food right on site and serve it from the bus.' Hugh nodded to the stairs. 'And we could use the upper deck when people wanted to talk privately or if anyone needed a place of safety.' I found my voice again. 'Could we really have this?' I asked Jackie. 'It would be a great asset to our work.' He laughed. 'I'm offering it to you. But there's one problem.' We looked at him. 'You'd need to find a bus driver, someone with a P.S.V. licence.' 'I have one,' I told him, grinning from ear to ear. It's not often I upstage Jackie Ross! How was he to know I'd once been a bus driver?

Typical of Jackie and Blythswood they finished the job in style, delivering the bus to us newly serviced, with a fresh MOT certificate, painted white and with Open Door Trust Glasgow's logo painted on it. The Big White Bus is now well known in Anderston where we reach out to over 150 homeless and needy people on the streets. We've had dealings with Jackie for some years, and that story is a good example of our co-operation. Jackie saw what we needed, knew he could help us, and did it right down to the logo. I praise God for Jackie Ross and men like him.

Working with Blythswood makes people aware of need and of the rest of the world. People all over Scotland, and in many other parts of the UK, collect clothes, blankets and lay aside dried and tinned food, fill shoe boxes at Christmas time and then take them to the Blythswood trucks as they go on their monthly collecting rounds. Others make a part of their homes, churches and business premises a dropping-off point for their local communities. Our charity shops have dedicated staff, again, most of them volunteers. And Deephaven relies on a large number of willing workers who go through the mountains of donations, separating them into their different kinds. Then there are those who wash, iron and repair clothes, the mechanics who service everything from small implements to the trucks themselves, those who go through thousands of toys to check for cleanliness and safety, the packers, the stackers, the lot. Drivers and others volunteer time, often holiday time, to deliver aid to countries where driving conditions can be bad. That's just the aid side of things. There is also Blythswood's literature ministry. Tracts have to be organised and distributed, correspondence courses sent out and marked when they are returned, Bibles and other literature need packed and posted, and the book-van and shops need to be stocked regularly. And there are all the administrative people too. Blythswood now has more paid workers but it could not manage without its army of volunteers. A whole book could be written about them. And those who support the work in prayer must not be forgotten.

James Campbell, Blythswood's Chief Executive
From the early 1990s an enormous relief aid effort developed, but I don't think Blythswood ever lost its focus as a tract society, though the situation in Eastern Europe meant that most of our resources were marshalled in the direction of aid for a time. I think that part of the reason for the changes of focus was Jackie himself, because his compassion is so great that he can't see a need without responding to it. He'd give the shirt off his back if someone needed it, regardless of the person's colour or creed.

Of course that kind of gut response doesn't always consider financial facts before springing into action.

I love Jackie's enthusiasm. When he phones and says he has something he wants to speak to me about, I feel a kind of excitement. I know he's going to present his latest idea. And I also know that if I don't take it on, he'll repackage it and present it again ... and again. The new book-van is an example. A few months ago he came in full of enthusiasm to get a book-van back on the road. Christian literature is his passion, and he was determined to see this project through. We decided to run with it as there was a van available that could be used. But it was a compromise. He wanted something bigger and more comfortable for customers. Two days later he was back on the subject, with the news that a library van, exactly what we needed, was on sale in Orkney. I hope I was kind, but I certainly was firm when I said that we'd have to wait a while, that finances weren't available. Jackie accepted my decision .... I thought. Before long, he got back to me with the news that the Stornoway Support Group would pay for the van and that someone had agreed to refurbish it so it wouldn't cost Blythswood anything. He set the whole thing up!

Working with Jackie is like being on a rollercoaster – you have to hang on. He is an inspiration, and a real mover and shaker. Part of his secret is that he motivates other people to do what he wants them to do. Of course things don't always work out, partly because Jackie is so optimistic that he sees the best in everyone and can make unwise decisions because of that. But he accepts his mistakes and is utterly forgiving when people let him down. He doesn't fudge issues, but he does deal with them graciously.

Donald MacLeod, former trustee of Blythswood
Jackie's greatest quality is his compassion for others. People who are broken in their bodies and minds, people who are weary because of the burdens they bear, and people whose wounds are self-inflicted - all these people I have seen cared for by Jackie and Elma. I have seen Jackie continue to help those whom others have given up on because they assessed them as incorrigible. I cannot recall him giving up on anybody. He has our Saviour's compassion.

And this compassion extends beyond simply listening sympathetically to the giving of practical support. If it is in his hand to give, he will give. I am one of those who was broken when he first met me and he, knowing that, took a risk and gave me a chance by employing me to work for Blythswood. Many people can testify to the way he gave not only first opportunities but also to the way he would stick by us.

Jackie cannot be properly understood unless you have some understanding of the remarkable stamina with which God has gifted him. I tried to keep pace with Jackie for a short while but gave up when I realised that there was no way I was endowed with his stamina.

Martin Cameron, one-time employee of Blythswood
Working with Jackie was a great privilege, going through good times and difficult times alongside

him, but with many laughs along the way! One of the features of his character that most impressed me, however, was his pastor's heart. This was evident on many occasions, and the following is one example. Someone who had let Jackie down badly had a run-in with the law. Jackie decided to stand by this person and wrote him a letter of support, which he showed me. In the letter, he spelt out the man's misdemeanours and the serious breach of trust which had taken place, but then went on to commend him for his hard work on behalf of his family, among other good points, assuring him that he would stand by him. He finished off the letter by confronting the man with his greatest fault, namely that he had sinned against his Creator and stood condemned before him, while clearly pointing him to the Saviour. All was done in scrupulous fairness, but with an overriding sense of concern and care for the individual, which is typical of Jackie.

Jackie's attitude to his present illness is, in many ways, no surprise to those who know him well. He has certainly been given the 'peace of God, which transcends all understanding', but, additionally he has a God-given grit and a life-long reluctance to sit down! My wife, Margaret, and I were in Applecross recently and called in on the Rosses on the way home. Elma was in the manse and Jackie was up at the new house, which was nearing completion. We drove up to the new house in gathering dusk, and, having not seen Jackie for a few weeks, we were slightly apprehensive at how much his illness might have affected him. When we arrived, we could just discern in the twilight a boiler-suited figure pushing a wheelbarrow full of heavy rocks uphill! It could only be one person, of course, and the picture sums up for me much of what makes Jackie the unique person he is.

James Campbell
Under Jackie's leadership Blythswood has come a long way since its early days in Glasgow. Its current projects include the new book-van and another of his bright ideas, a mail order book club. We have twenty four charity shops and five book shops. There are depots in Rochester, which is strategic for the Channel, Bristol, Glasgow and Ballyclare. The organisation works with sixty-eight full or part-time staff and an army of volunteers. In 2000 we sent out the equivalent of 121 articulated loads of aid, which is approximately 1,500 tonnes. This went to eighteen countries. Had we bought the aid we sent it would have cost between £8.5 million and £10 million. Most of our aid goes to Romania, Bulgaria and Albania, but in 2000 we sent help to fifteen other countries too. We support numerous projects run by Christian groups in many countries, and we have some major projects of our own.

The Daniel Centre, in the city of Cluj in Romania, opened in June 2000. It provides a home for eight ex-orphanage teenagers who otherwise would be living on the streets. The challenge for the staff is to build and maintain a culture of parental affection towards the boys which does not comes easily in a society as dysfunctional as post-communist Romania. After two years, three of the original boys are sufficiently mature to live independently. Two of them are holding down outside jobs and are doing well in them, the third is a steady worker within the Daniel Centre project. A fourth is considering a move to another part of Eastern Europe and a fifth has returned to his parents. All eight boys have a future. Before the Daniel Centre opened the best they could have hoped for was an existence.

Robi Man, one of the first boys to live at the Daniel Centre
Before I came to the Centre, life was very difficult for me. It was hard because I had no friends and nobody to talk to. I also had nowhere to live as I had been brought up in orphanages all of my life. I didn't have anything to live for. I heard about the Daniel Centre through a woman who knew one of the house parents. I came to see the place and immediately wanted to stay. I'm a Christian now and I was baptised not long ago. I'm one of the first boys to take this step. Before I knew Jesus I was lonely and had no-one to talk too. But now I not only have Jesus but I have all my church friends too. I enjoy going to church. I'm involved in the youth meetings as well as the choir. If I hadn't had the opportunity to come here to the Daniel Centre I wouldn't have had a good job or had people to care for me. I am a very happy person.

Finlay MacKenzie
My wife and I went out with Jackie to the opening of the Daniel Centre. It was a joy and an answer to prayer that he was able to go, especially as he had just completed his radiotherapy the week before.

Sometimes Romanians' fondness for him almost verges on hero worship and he finds that profoundly embarrassing. I believe that going to the opening helped Jackie at what was a very difficult time. It was a dream come true for him. The Centre is quite a responsibility for Blythswood. It's one thing delivering a load of aid, it's quite another being responsible for these boys twenty four hours a day, seven days a week. We are locked into that now and, with God's help, we have to make it work.

James Campbell

Project Joseph aims to 'rescue Romanian orphans by agricultural means.' It is run by Calin Gabor, a medical graduate and social worker, who is the son of a farmer. His wife, also a social worker, is experienced in working with orphans. They aim to provide training, supervision and jobs in agriculture for orphans who would otherwise be on the streets. It is estimated that there are 200 unemployed young people from orphanages in their area of Bihor. An interest-free loan from Blythswood has enabled them to invest in greenhouses, an irrigation system, tools, and a van. The project's name comes from Joseph in the Old Testament, a Hebrew slave who saved a nation from famine.

Talita Kum, which began in September 2001, is a pioneering venture in child care in Jimbolia, south western Romania. Adrian Popa, the instigator and leader of the project, is one of several students Blythswood has supported through theological college. Romanian schools close at midday and children may be left to fend for themselves, without food, until a parent returns from work. Talita Kum offers a six hour programme from lunch until early evening, including a meal, two hours of tutoring and help with homework, games, and Christian teaching. Blythswood bought a large bungalow to house the project. Adrian plans to open a charity shop nearby to help offset the running costs.

These projects and hundreds of others that Blythswood supports are all part of a jigsaw. The complete picture is known only to God. Just as Blythswood was encouraged to hear from a young minister in Nigeria who traced his Christian influence to one of the Society's tracts his father read when he was a child, we trust that the fruit of Blythswood's ministry will be produced for decades to come. Meanwhile, we try to do what Jackie has always done, that is to meet whatever need presents itself to us.

Despite Jackie's illness he's exhausting us still. Until the Lord stops him, he'll keep going at speed. When he was in a great deal of pain recently he phoned to say that he wasn't too good and that he'd have to cancel some engagements. That was on a Monday. The following day he was a bit better. On Wednesday he went to Stornoway on Blythswood business, returning home on Friday to pick up Elma and fly to London for a prayer breakfast on Saturday morning. That lunchtime he opened a shop in Cromer, preached there twice on Sunday, then flew to Belfast on Monday. He worked there Monday and Tuesday before flying home to attend a presbytery and to chair a conference at the end of the week.

It has been an immense privilege working with him over the last few years. There has been wonderful fun and some grief too. He's a wise man, and very down to earth. I'm grateful to have had the benefit of his experience. He often says, 'James, don't do it this way. I've tried it and it was a mistake.' It takes a big man to recognise his mistakes and an even bigger one to admit them. Jackie is that man. And Jackie wouldn't be half the man he is without Elma.

Donald Macleod
There was an occasion on which I found I needed to speak plainly to Jackie on a certain subject. And although what I had to say affected him so much that he left our meeting ashen-faced and sombre, it did not then, nor has it ever since, changed his attitude to me. The accepting spirit in which Jackie took what I had to say remains with me as an abiding lesson as to how I, as a believer, ought to respond to rebuke or correction from my brothers or sisters in Christ.

Jackie is a man who is loved by many – including myself – because he loves people. He is a man to whom you would go if you were in dire straits, knowing that he and Elma would always be willing to help and would never close their door upon you. It is that openness and engagement with others which testifies most clearly to me of the love of God in Christ Jesus our Lord at work in the lives of Jackie and Elma.

11

O do not cast me off, when as
old age doth overtake me;
And when my strength decayed is,
then do not thou forsake me.
(Psalm 71:9)

Lochcarron

Helen Murchison, Lochcarron Community Councillor
I've known Jackie since he and Elma came to
Lochcarron. They are down-to-earth people, with
no airs and graces. The folk in the village are more
likely to meet Jackie dressed in dungarees and
looking for a pound of nails than to meet him
wearing a dog collar and suit. Maybe that's partly
why he's so approachable. It doesn't matter what
denomination you are, or if you don't go to church
at all, the Rosses are still interested in you. Jackie
and I served on the Community Council together
for years and were involved in all sorts of discussions
and decisions, from the state of the roads to funding
for the playgroup. Some ministers don't get involved
in such day-to-day things, but Jackie is a man with a

big heart and his concern is for the whole community in all its aspects. Working with him is good fun. He has a great sense of humour and he puts it to good use in tense situations. He's got us out of many a fix in that way.

Over the years Jackie has contributed much to life in Lochcarron, but the most notable of all the projects he has spearheaded is the Howard Doris Centre, which provides care in the village for those who need extra support on the short or long-term but who don't need the hi-tech medical care they would get if they were to go to Inverness, over sixty miles away, and our nearest hospital. At first this seemed a totally impossible dream but Jackie never let go of it. Right from the very beginning we met obstacles but he never let them get at him. 'The Lord will provide,' he told us often. And we didn't believe it. But the whole thing did come together and it's a wonderful resource for the village. There are many local folk, especially among the older people, who are deeply grateful to Jackie Ross for his vision and determination, and his faith too.

David Murray, Doctor, Lochcarron
I first came across Jackie Ross in 1985, just after I took over the medical practice here. There was a call to attend what sounded like a serious road traffic accident at Achnasheen. I set off, travelling as fast as the road allowed. Not far along the road I caught up on a blue Mini which was travelling equally fast. Passing it on a long straight, I raced on to Achnasheen with the Mini right behind me all the way. When I looked in the mirror and saw the driver

was wearing a dog collar, I assumed he was the priest and that he was rushing to give the last rites at the scene of the accident. When I arrived I pulled in off the road and left room for the Mini to park. But it didn't, it raced past heading for Easter Ross. It wasn't the priest, it was Jackie Ross in a rush as usual. Thankfully the accident turned out to be not very serious at all.

At the end of the eighties I was looking for land on which to build a new surgery, and I had my eye on a field in the village. One day, as I drove past the field, I noticed Jackie and another man in it, obviously eyeing it up for some project. I parked the car and went to see what they were up to. Jackie introduced me to his companion, Mike Cairns of Age Concern, and explained that he'd invited him to consider the field as a potential site on which to build a centre for the care of the area's older people. 'Come along for a coffee and we can talk it over,' Jackie invited. That's how the biggest thing to happen in the village for years came about.

The problem Jackie had identified was one I was very aware of. There was no nursing home in the area and folk who were no longer able to live in their own homes with support had to go to Inverness. People who had no need of sophisticated medical intervention were taken from their own homes, sometimes from remote crofts, to acute receiving wards in Raigmore Hospital. They didn't need to be there, all they needed was more support. It was also a source of great sadness to me as a doctor to have to send people suffering from a terminal illness away from their families and friends when, with more local resources, they could have been looked after here in Lochcarron.

When people went away like that it was as though they had died, even though some of them, especially stroke patients and others with long-term needs, lived for years after leaving the area to be cared for elsewhere. Because they were mainly older people, those whom they'd known all their days were often unable to visit. It was a very unsatisfactory situation and it caused a great deal of heartache. Couples who had been together for forty or more years were separated for no good medical reason and so were bereft of each other before either had died. That was the need Jackie identified, and in true Jackie Ross style he did something about it.

His first approach was to the Community Council, of which he was then Chairman, with the suggestion that they should look for ways of providing for the needs of the area's older people. There was already some sheltered housing; Elma Ross was the relief warden, and the usual nursing services. The Community Council agreed with Jackie that there was a real need for some kind of centre, but felt that it was beyond their scope. The District Council was then approached for assistance and the Chief Executive caught the vision. Before long there were three main players: Highland Council Social Work Department, Albyn Housing and the Strathcarron Project. A momentum developed and for a while we were swept along, but two or three years into the project it was in danger of not fulfilling all its original aims. Jackie, Helen Murchison and I decided that we were going to keep the focus where we wanted it to be and see the thing through to its end.

Working with Jackie was an interesting experience, in all kinds of ways! He had an immense faith that things would work out. Several times it looked as though money was going to be a problem, and each time he would tell us that money was the last thing we had to worry about. At one point, when there looked to be a shortfall of over £100,000, there was a suggestion that we should call a temporary halt. 'We'll get the money,' Jackie told us. 'Just keep going. Money's no problem.' It wasn't easy to believe him but he was right, we got a European grant! Jackie has an unorthodox way of going about things. He gets things done, then works out how to do them afterwards. That's landed him in hot water from time to time, but it's the kind of mindset that does the impossible.

What started off as Jackie's dream in 1989 became a reality in 1996 when the Howard Doris Centre opened, providing what the village needed: permanent accommodation for eight local people who have need for extra support, two medical beds for acute care of patients, (who do not need the technical resources of a large hospital), two beds for respite care, and a day care facility for over thirty people a day. The local library is also part of the complex.

Jackie has made me think. However, sometimes my thoughts haven't been all that holy because his determination which gets things done, also from time to time makes him so stubborn that he isn't even able to hear another point of view, let alone take notice of it. But I reckon that's a small price to pay for the privilege of working with him. I hope I've not copied Jackie's stubbornness, but I certainly have tried to copy his attitude to getting things done. Working with him has shown me that if you stick at something tenaciously, refusing to change your focus and not allowing yourself to be deflected by problems and red tape, you do get things done, even things that seem almost impossible at the beginning.

When I first knew Jackie he was as compassionate and practical as he is now, but I don't think he was living in the real world. It was as though he was blinkered about some things that were going on in the community. He has changed and I think he does have as good a knowledge as anyone of what is happening locally, both good and bad. It seems to me that the tradition he came from encouraged people to shut their eyes against what they would call 'the world', and I think he did that. The change in him was gradual but I think it makes him a more effective minister.

Jackie Ross is a fascinating mixture. He's a mover and shaker who is fundamentally driven by his faith but doesn't now seem to be constrained by it. He is a man of huge inner conviction, honour and compassion, always willing to get stuck right in and do things rather than pontificating about what should be done. I'm full of admiration for Jackie, and for Elma too.

Ishbel Mackinnon, Manager, Howard Doris Centre

I come from Lochcarron but I worked away for many years. I was very aware of the needs of the older people in the area and the job as manager of the new Centre appealed to me. The interview was unlike any other I've ever had. Jackie knew what my roots were, but the others did not. For the entire length of the interview I was aware of his amusement as the others tried to work out who I was from my knowledge of the local situation. He wanted them to find out for themselves, and he enjoyed watching them do so. That first meeting with Jackie was typical. He's efficient and fun with it. I got the job. When I heard the news I phoned and asked Jackie when he wanted me to start. 'No need to rush,' he told me. 'Just when you're ready.' I thought that was unusual, but I've since discovered that Jackie does work in unusual ways.

When I moved back to Lochcarron, the Howard Doris Centre was half built and my office was a portacabin. That's where Jackie and I had our first meeting as Chairman and Centre Manager. The sum total of our 'office equipment' was a blank notebook, three pens and a wee posy of flowers put there by Catriona who worked in the Blythswood office. We spent three hours together discussing the way forward, then he went away. That was me installed and inducted and I was left to get on with it. For someone like me who was used to working within defined structures and procedures, this was a new experience.

I've now worked with Jackie Ross for six years and I've never worked with anyone like him! I've learned many things from him. For example, when something goes wrong he always seems to find a way of turning it for the best, even making it seem that the problem was a good thing because it moved the situation forward. It hasn't always been easy though, partly because I never know Jackie's agenda as it's usually so far ahead of mine. I discuss things with him thinking they relate to the immediate situation, only to discover that he's addressing a long- term objective I've not yet heard about. Probably the aspect of working with Jackie Ross which I've found most difficult at times is the problem of saying 'no' to him. He carries people along with him in such a way that they feel they are letting him down if they say 'no' to his plans. And when they do manage to say the word, he doesn't even hear it. Over the years I've developed a way of compromising with him.

Jackie and Elma are a wonderful couple, totally complementary. He is the visionary and she is the more practical one of the two. One thing they have in common is their compassion, another is a great sense of humour and fun. It's said that all work and no play makes Jack a dull boy, but Jackie and Elma seem to get through a phenomenal amount of work while remaining interesting, entertaining and amusing people. Just how much of a visionary Jackie is came home to me when I found myself welcoming visitors to the Howard Doris Centre from many parts of Scotland and as far away as Sweden and Russia. It is a unique development and one which other places envy. While I know that the Project was the work of a team of people, I believe that it would never have come about had it not been for Jackie Ross. He saw the vision, and he held on to it regardless. The other people who came on board did a power of work to make the Project materialise.

Typical of Jackie, when he wrote the Foreword to the Report on the Project, he concluded with, 'To all who contributed with help and advice in any way we express our thanks. Above all we give thanks to God, to whom the Project was committed through prayer as each phase developed.' Jackie seems to see even practical things are in some ways spiritual, the Howard Doris Centre included. But he doesn't force his Christianity on other people. There is worship in the Centre each Sunday but there is no pressure to attend. As for worship on other days - I think he would like to have seen that as part of the programme, but he has never pushed for it. Jackie is a tolerant man when it comes to respecting other people's views, but everyone in the village knows where he stands.

Working with Jackie Ross has made a great impression on me. Probably due to his influence I try to think before I speak, though I don't always succeed in doing so. He and I are very different people and while I owe so much to him I also have my own professional integrity. We have differed and learned from our differences. I came to Lochcarron with management skills, I suppose that's why I got the job, but I've learned a different kind of management from him, even if some of his methods are unorthodox and not to be copied. These last six years have been hard work and a great privilege. And the reward for it all is to see those who use the Centre able to remain in their own community, with their own folk, for as long as possible and often until the end of their lives.

Mairi Forsyth

I used to live in a sheltered house in Lochcarron but the time came when I was unable to cope there on my own. I have very bad arthritis and other problems too, and I had frequent falls. The Howard Doris Centre was built at just the right time for me. It was God's provision for my needs. If the Centre was not here I'd be in Inverness or Invergordon, away from the place that has been my home. At my age it is not easy to cope with new places and new people. It is a thousand times better to be here in my own community than away being looked after by strangers, no matter how kind they are. I was in hospital not so long ago in Inverness but it was good to be home. The Centre is my home. Although most of my friends have passed away or are old like myself, I know the families of the people here and we have things we can talk about.

I've known Jackie Ross since he came to Lochcarron, and Elma too. If it had not been for him and Dr David Murray the Centre would never have been built. This place was his idea and he is still very involved in it. Elma is a nurse in the Centre. They have both helped to look after me in my old age. I thank God for them.

12

Yea, though I walk in death's dark vale,
yet will I fear none ill:
For thou art with me; and thy rod
and staff me comfort still.
(Psalm 23:4)

Living with Cancer

August and September 1999 were due to be busy
months. Sarah's first baby was due. Jason was to have
his twenty-first birthday and then be married. Elma
had to finish sewing the bridesmaid's dress for the
wedding and then do some preparation for a course in
palliative-care nursing she was due to start at the
beginning of October. If nothing else had happened
it would still have been an eventful month.

Elma
Having had investigations earlier in the year, Jackie
went to hospital for another examination three
weeks before Jason's wedding. We were not
expecting significant news and I didn't go to

Inverness with him. When Jackie phoned to say that he needed major surgery for the removal of a tumour, and that the surgeon wanted to see us both together the following day, I was shocked. My reaction was to go into busy mode, telling the children and Jackie's family, cancelling my course and letting my manager know I would need time off work. It was prayer meeting night. I told our elder the news and he shared it with the others there. Our people were shocked too because Jackie always seemed to be so active and fit that no-one suspected he was unwell. There was anxiety mixed with calm at the meeting. After everyone left, Jason and I drove through to Inverness to see Jackie. That night, when I went to bed in Philip and Marianne's home in Inverness, my mind was in overdrive, busy with disjointed, ineffective thinking. Putting together prayer sentences didn't work but I knew that this was what my Father in heaven had planned for us and that he would not leave or forsake us, whatever lay ahead. Sleep seemed far away but at last the simple thought came, 'Well, if this is the event that is going to part Jackie and me it will only be for a little while anyway.' The reality of everlasting life flooded in and I fell asleep. That was enough for that night. Many times since I have needed the Lord to strengthen me with reminders of more of his promises. And he has.

The following day Jackie and I met with the consultant. The family zoomed into Inverness and we all began to absorb the reality of what was happening. Jackie's admission was scheduled for the day after Jason and Wilma's wedding and the operation for the day after that. Meantime, it was back to work as usual for Jackie. A couple of days later he was fulfilling a preaching engagement in Aberdeen. For myself, it was back to my sewing. I had cancelled my course, but I knew that my Lord was taking me on a different education experience, but not necessarily one less useful for me in my work.

I had problems for a few years before my cancer was discovered, and by then it was well advanced. The day I got the news, there was another man there who seemed to have the same diagnosis. We felt so sad for him because he was alone and did not know, or want to know, God or the comfort that comes through 'casting your care on him'. Right from the start Elma has come with me to all hospital appointments and the whole experience has drawn us closer together. It's a strange thing that people often say 'if anything happens to my husband' or 'if anything happens to my wife', because it's not 'if' but 'when'. Death will come and will usually take one of a couple first. For us the realisation that it's likely to be just round the corner has made every day precious. If we had not shared the experience we would have missed out on that blessing.

Elma
Within the space of a few days we celebrated the birth of Sarah and Alasdair's little daughter, Emily, and Jason's twenty-first birthday. Although the forthcoming surgery was never very far from our minds we were able to carry on much as normal. On the morning of the wedding, as well as packing

our wedding gear into the car, we had to take Jackie's case for going into hospital the next day. It was an unusual combination. Jackie and I set out from Lochcarron with Lois and eight-month-old Matthew in the back seat of the car. Eight miles from Lochcarron the car went out of control on a corner, rolled down a bank and hit a tree. I remember hearing Lois asking if I was all right, and asking Jackie the same thing. We both said we were. Then Matthew screamed, really screamed. What a wonderful sound that was.

Other cars were also travelling to the wedding. In the one right behind us was the nurse manager of the Howard Doris Centre. She and her husband took control of the scene and other drivers flew into action, sending for the emergency services. Shocked, cut, bruised and in a mess, Jackie, Lois and Matthew were helped out of the car. From the glimpse I had got of Jackie I knew there was blood all over his face and I wanted to get to him. But I was stuck, and squashed in a tiny space with my head trapped in something. I could feel my self drifting and I felt that I would lose consciousness if I didn't get free quickly. The voices I could hear in the background sounded as if they were a thousand miles away but I had heard the words 'smoke' and 'fire'. I needed to get out. With help and determination I managed to get out of the car but was passing out as I did so. Although I felt weak and in great pain I was filled with thankfulness that we were all alive. The doctor seemed to be there very quickly and I discovered that the screech of an ambulance siren can be a welcome sound.

Living where we do has many benefits. That day it was comforting to know the doctor, the nurses, the paramedics and the firemen. I was surrounded by familiar faces. My boss, Ishbel, was down on her knees beside me, her professionalism shelved, calling me, 'Elma, pet'! My nephew, Duncan, who is a part-time fireman, was at the other side reassuring me, 'You're all right, Auntie.' When Jackie is in shock he rushes around trying to do what is required to sort the situation, when what he needs is someone to sit him down quietly. I wondered where he was. Was someone with him? Later I learned that in a typical desire to resolve the problem, he had persuaded someone to take him home to get another car to get us to the wedding. That plan was abandoned once Lois rescued him and took care of him. I was taken by ambulance to Garve, from where I was taken by helicopter to hospital in Inverness. I was treated in Accident and Emergency before being admitted for a week with injuries to my shoulder, hip and a lung. The wedding was held back for about half an hour but though neither of us was able to be there we were glad it proceeded. Lois and Matthew arrived at the church as the company came out and Jackie, after he was checked at the hospital, made it for a time to the reception. I was unable to be there at all. Were I to have let my thoughts dwell on that or to do so even now I could become immensely sad. Instead, when I think back to that day, the memory of the Lord's goodness and presence remains. As in Psalm 103 I can say to my soul, 'Bless God the Lord and do not forget his gracious benefits to you, because he has graciously forgiven all your iniquities and has healed and relieved your pains.'

The day after the wedding Jackie joined me in Raigmore Hospital. His room was a few doors down from mine. I could see that he was shaken from the effects of the day before and in need of rest. Next day Jackie was in theatre for five hours for what the surgeon described as 'a difficult operation'. That evening when someone took me in a wheelchair to visit him, he was recovering from the anaesthesia and gave me a warm welcome, eager to know how I was rather than tell me how he himself was. He made rapid progress in his recovery and three days before his planned discharge he asked if he could get dressed. Of course he could. 'And can I put my shoes on?' he asked. He himself expected the implication of his question to be understood and made for outside, for the bus shelter. As he waited there for the next bus, a friend of ours, a policeman who was at the hospital in the course of his duties, spotted him and offered him a lift.

I had been discharged a few days earlier and was staying at Philip's home in Inverness. Marianne, my daughter-in-law, and I were sitting chatting when her door bell rang. I saw the astonishment on her face as she went into the hall and looked through the glass door. Yes, there was Jackie. It was lovely to see him but I was relieved when Philip set off with him in the car, back to the hospital. Sure enough they had wondered where he had gone but all was well.

The pathology result showed the need for

chemotherapy. I was pleased about that, hoping it was a safeguard, but Jackie was disappointed. Six sessions of treatment followed over the next twelve weeks during which Jackie got on with life. He preached, visited, worked for Blythswood and supervised the building of our new home in Lochcarron. We planned to spend our retirement there. Often I found myself wondering if we would ever live in the house together. Within a month of finishing his chemotherapy, in January 2000, Jackie developed severe pain in his lower back. Various medications relieved it temporarily but in March a bone scan was done. Both of us knew the result before it came back. Jackie's cancer had spread to his sacrum, the big flat bone at the end of his spine. He was given morphine as his pain was by then persistent and severe.

Radiotherapy was carried out five days a week for several weeks, with Jackie usually driving to Inverness each day for his treatment and then driving back home again. That made life reasonably normal and he was able to crash out on his own bed when he felt like it. He had very high doses of radiotherapy and its side-effects continued to make him feel progressively ill for three weeks after the completion of the course. Even so, a week after finishing radiotherapy we went to Romania for the opening of the Daniel Centre!

We set off with some apprehension, lots of morphine and odds and ends supplied by our local medical centre to cope with possible eventualities on the way. The reactions to his intention to go were funny – some folks were cross that he would be so silly, others afraid for him and a few shared his enthusiasm. For myself, I suppose that dogged determination that has often tried me to the limits is also one of the characteristics that I love and admire in my husband's personality. Most importantly many prayed for us while we were on that trip. It was a struggle but we were glad to be there for so special an event. Each day Jackie mustered the strength to visit the places and projects in which Blythswood works in Cluj Napoca, ignoring the fatigue and pain as we bumped along in a van on Romania's still pot-holed roads. Meeting friends, old and new, he and they enthused together about the progress made with the work, providing each other with mutual encouragement. And then to see the young lads at the Daniel Centre, so pleased with and proud of their new home, was a great joy. A coach load of Blythswood workers and volunteers had come from Scotland for the occasion and Romanian friends gathered to join us. It was worth all the effort.

Later, in September, we were able to go with Ali, Sarah and little Emily to France for a holiday but by then the old pain which had diminished was recurring. Two months on another scan showed that the tumour, which had been reduced by radiotherapy, had increased again. Since then he has had no further scans. We don't know how the cancer is progressing . We have no assurance of containment but we do have the assurance that God is working all things together for our good, as he has promised for those who love him. And yes, we do love him. We love him and we praise him for coming into our lives and rescuing us from our sin. Jackie is still working, still ministering whenever he can and still living with enthusiasm. For the present, most of the time, life is almost normal, partly because of his ability to get up and go. That is his God-given temperament and it would be wrong for us to use it as a standard for any other ill person. But we have to ask if our view of 'normal' has perhaps changed. For myself I have to ask, 'What was life like before cancer?' One adapts and changes. We're not in denial of what's happening. The reality is always there and some days are hard. We thank God for morphine and that Jackie has been able to tolerate it well enough to allow him to function a lot of the time. We have outstanding medical help in our own community and have recourse to specialist attention when we need it.

We told our family right away that my cancer was terminal, and we've kept them informed of everything that's been happening. It was very moving for me to see their reactions and to feel their love. I felt a responsibility to help them cope with the situation, looking on it as more of a problem for them than for me. I suppose that's something to do with being a husband, a father and a minister. I felt I almost had to apologise for being ill. But my illness is something God has allowed. It's the Lord's doing and my priority is to help them through it, though I do see that one day it will possibly be they who have to help me.

Jason
When we heard that Dad had cancer it was horrible.
Cancer only happens in other families. It took a
while to sink in and we hoped that the tumour would
be removed and that would be the end of it. So it
was terrible to hear eventually that he had bone
cancer, worse than the first time because it's
incurable. I was in the car with Philip when we
heard, and he's a good person to have around in a
time like that. I asked him if it was just a matter of
time and he said that it is always just a matter of
time. We're glad that Dad has remained in such
good health for so long. It's been quite unexpected
and a real bonus for all of us. Some people suggest
that he's doing well because he has a good spirit
and battles on, but it's not that at all. Dad's still
here as an answer to prayer.

I'm an enthusiast, optimistic and not too easily put
down. That's how I've lived with cancer. In some ways
this last couple of years has been such a good time.
The family has been amazing and I've enjoyed the
grandchildren so much. Having them at this stage in
my life is a real blessing. And cancer has introduced
me to many people I'd not otherwise have met. One
man in hospital said, 'Hello, what's wrong with you?'
'I've got cancer,' I told him. 'Did you ever drive a Model
T Ford?' he asked. I said I had not. Then for about
five minutes he spoke non-stop on his experience of
driving Model T Fords. He put up a complete barrier
because he couldn't face the idea of cancer, his or mine.

That's how some react. In others it opens doors, opens hearts.

When, after surgery, I learned that I needed chemotherapy to stop the cancer's advance, I thought I would need to get my life a bit more ordered, organise a good reading scheme, develop my private devotions, get into a better spiritual state. So I struggled to do that. Then the thought came to me very powerfully, 'All you need is Christ.' That's so wonderful, so complete. It changed my devotions into times of thanksgiving and love to God. That has made this a happy time, with a greater appreciation that all I need is Christ. It is through him that I have forgiveness of sin, peace in my conscience and strength for every day the Lord gives me. What a relief! When I was converted and delivered from so great a death, it was all of grace. And my trust for the future is the same - it's all of grace.

The new appreciation of Christ meant that a stress was taken away. It showed me that the main thing is to give thanks. Since I've had cancer people have prayed for me to be healed. But the big thing in the whole experience is that the Lord is in it, and he is teaching me, teaching me to trust in him. It is much more glorious to think that the Lord is giving me wisdom and new insights into himself than it would be if I were healed. What I'm learning is for eternity; healing would only be for a time. I think cancer has given me a focus on eternal things. For example, so many people have come to see me since they knew I was ill, some have even come from abroad though that threw me a bit, and I want to be useful to each one of them in an eternal way. They come to say goodbye to me in case they don't see me again, but that's not what I want to focus on. They come feeling sad, and I see their visits as a gift from the Lord. Some of them have found that hard to cope with.

The visits that mean most are those from our children and grandchildren. We quite often have family worship together when we sing, read and everyone prays. My health is part of the subject of their prayers and it is so heartwarming to hear them praying with an anticipation of heaven. It gives me a real sense that although it seems that I'm shortly to die we are not going to be parted forever. It was wonderful when the children were converted, but it is as though I'm experiencing that joy again now as I think of being together with all the family in heaven. Somehow the children's response to my going home to heaven affected me differently from when I met it from some of my friends.

Lois

Initially when I heard Dad's cancer was terminal I didn't pray for his healing. I left it to the others to do that. I think I was afraid of believing he would be healed in case it didn't happen. But it became easier to pray about healing and to a degree he has been healed. I cringe with a kind of fear when I hear people praying that Dad should be given a little more time because for me a little isn't enough. And when they pray that he'll be here for some event or other, I long to tell them that I want him after that's over. It has helped us all that Dad's been able to go on almost normally for so much longer than anyone expected and I don't now live with constant fear. Some nights I phone home and he has gone to bed in terrible pain and then next day when I phone he's in Glasgow!

One of the wonderful answers to prayer over Dad's illness was to do with their new home. It was being built for their retirement when Dad took ill. The day Mum and Dad moved into the house, Andrew, the joiner and our friend, told us that about a year before, when the house was in its early stages, Dad was there with our son, Matthew, trying to do things at the bottom of the site. He wasn't well at all. Looking out the window seeing him struggle, Andrew fell to his knees and prayed that Dad would be spared long enough to see Matthew running around in the new house. He saw that day and he's seen it a few times since. It's precious to us that Dad and Mum are having a time together in their new home. It means that when he dies it will have been their home, not just Mum's. That seems a little thing but it's important.

Mum has supported all of us, not just Dad. She's practical and a competent nurse. In a way that's made it easier for us as we are all content to leave the responsibility of Dad's care in her hands. For as long as I can remember Mum has been called out to be with people in the village when they were ill or dying, and that goes back to long before she went back to nursing. That will make it easier for him if a time comes when Mum has to do a lot of practical caring for him.

Friends have sometimes tried to comfort me by saying how wonderful it will be to get to heaven. Of course I understand them saying that and I have probably said it myself to believers whose death may have been imminent. But I would think twice about it now. It can be a glib way of avoiding the reality of the physical and emotional pain that may have to be confronted before reaching heaven and the joy of meeting the Lord. For a time I found that kind of thinking quite oppressive. I hope to go to heaven. I expect to go to heaven. But it's wonderful to be here on earth. I believe it is a blessing from God to love life, to want to live it to the full and to enjoy time here working for him. I'm still caught up with the wonder of things to do here. My focus is still set firmly on the privilege of the Lord's company here. Occasionally over the years when life was full of hassles I would wish I could get away and escape to heaven. But that wasn't a godly longing; it was a weariness with myself, the bother I could get into and the problems on the way. Cancer hasn't done that to me yet, but I believe that I'll be given a right frame of mind when that time comes. The joiner who was working on the new home Elma and I have just moved into spoke to me one day. 'I've been reading Martyn Lloyd-Jones,' he said, 'and Lloyd-Jones said to his wife one day, "You can stop praying for me to recover now. I'm ready to go."' I've not reached that stage yet. That was the joiner telling the minister a thing or two!

Sarah
Sometimes I hurt for Dad just now because he's often in so much pain. A few weeks ago I went up

to Lochcarron with friends from France. Dad came through to greet them but was in so much pain he soon had to go to bed. The colour had drained from his face and he was very weak. Seeing his illness cause a sudden change in Dad's appearance can be quite frightening. Cancer itself hasn't changed him at all. He talks quite openly about what's happening and about how he's feeling. Dad and Mum's accident on the day of Jason's wedding was a big thing for us. His operation was to be in two days. We were worried about his health and then Mum came out of the accident with more injuries than he did. God used that to remind me that he gives and takes life at his appointed time. Emily was less than two weeks old at the time of Jason and Wilma's wedding, so between that and the accident I probably missed out on some of the finer details of the day. But I do have one outstanding memory. Suddenly applause filled the dining room. I couldn't see what it was all about but my cousin who was sitting beside me turned my head. There was Dad. His face was cut and bruised but never was I so glad to see him.

Jeremy

When Dad was diagnosed with cancer I grieved so much. I thought, 'That's it. He's dead.' I think that because I grieved so much then I'm more able to enjoy the time I have with him now. Sometimes I get excited about Dad's situation and the way he's coping with it. I know that when he dies it will be painful for me, but part of what he's taught me is that it will be all right. One of the hardest things for me since he became ill was listening to him preaching at a service in Lochcarron. His text was 'In my Father's house are many mansions.' Listening to him was like being on an emotional rollercoaster. One minute I would be dreading the thought of life without him and the next minute rejoicing with him that in the Father's house there are many mansions and a place there for him.

The family's consolation is that we are all in God's hands. They didn't ever see my illness as anything other than being in God's hands, God's good hands. I had a great number of people phoning me and coming to visit, and many of them prayed for my healing. I've had phone calls from Sierra Leone with speaking in tongues, rebuking the devil and casting out the demon of cancer too. These folk came covering me with their love and concern but I felt sorry about the burden they had. I remember coming off the phone one Sunday evening so heavy-hearted. The person who had called prayed over the phone for me but all his shouting and casting out of demons only made me feel sad for him. He didn't seem able to see cancer as having anything to do with my heavenly Father preparing me for heaven, preparing me to be more like Jesus. I know all illness is the result of the Fall, but I don't see my cancer as being directly from the devil. For a time I hardly had space to think about the subject at all, so many people came telling me this or that that my mind felt bombarded. I believe that there's a real danger in attributing every problem and difficulty to Satan. That's a great and terrible mistake.

Some came and asked how the Lord could do this after all I had done for him. I felt like screaming. It's not like that. They were trying to comfort me but it was no comfort. It made me feel troubled for them. I was able to address this with some who said it, but not with others, because their beliefs were so firmly fixed in their minds. Others commented that if Adam hadn't fallen then we'd not have all these troubles. But he did, and we do, and God in his great mercy uses it. My thoughts went along various lines. I questioned the opportunities I've missed and the mistakes I've made. My reaction was to want to rush around frantically to make up for it all, to put right all the wrongs. But no, I discovered that I had to commit even my missed opportunities and my mistakes to the Lord and rest on the fact that redemption in Christ is so great that it covers all of them, every one.

Elma chose a psalm to be sung at our wedding that includes the verse, 'My sins and faults of youth do thou, O Lord, forget: after thy mercy think on me, and for thy goodness great'. I can look back and see all that I've done and not done, my pride, my arrogance, the wrong attitudes I've harboured, and the things I don't even want to mention. Somehow, facing the end of my life here on earth has brought home to me the full truth of the words of our wedding psalm. I can come to the Lord with my past in a wonderful way, and I can leave it all with him. He has dealt with it already. What I've to do is to accept the fact that the transaction is complete. That's such a relief!

Although I have put the past behind me, I still have things to do in the future, however short that future will be. I hope to have the opportunity to say thank you and goodbye to so many people, but that's a difficult one as I don't know who I'll see again. I could be saying thank you and goodbye to the same people over and over again. Maybe that wouldn't be a bad thing! Some friends have talked about the future with me, saying that they've prayed asking God to add years to my life, and they've rejoiced in the answer to their prayers. While I value their support, that puts me in a difficult position. It makes me feel a failure when I have pain or other signs that years are not being added to my life. Some days I have a struggle with pain, but I also have a struggle with that kind of thinking. I do look forward to a future here on earth, but I look forward to the end of the day, the end of the week, maybe the end of the month. I don't look for extended years though I'll be glad if they are given. I've often preached about living each day at a time in dependence on God; now I really do.

Donald Stewart, elder, Lochcarron
There is a sadness in the congregation and community about Mr Ross's illness, especially as he is sometimes in severe pain. But we are glad his ministry is continuing and expanding to take in his fellow sufferers, with the realisation that God gives a man his ministry in whatever circumstances he is in. There is work to do and we pray that he will have the grace to do it well.

Having incurable cancer has reinforced my thinking. I was once or twice criticised by friends who said that in my preaching I didn't seem to move beyond the subjects of repentance and faith, that I didn't have much to say on holy living. There was truth in that. But I focus now more and more on these two. Repenting wasn't something I did only in the 1960s, and never again since, and it's my belief that it's from repentance that holy living springs. Someone has said that we should keep short accounts with God. That's what I'm trying to do. And that's about repentance and it can only help towards holy living.

Marion

Seeing Jackie now makes the family sad, but his attitude to his illness and the grace that has shone through in the midst of the challenge of it all is a great comfort to us. It's one thing to speak about Christianity; it's quite another to live it out when the going gets tough. But Jackie is doing that. He seems to be using his cancer as a means of ministry and that's a brave thing to do as it sets him up to be knocked down if the cancer gets on top of him.

Sheena

Jackie's illness was a big blow to us all. When I heard that his cancer was terminal and that he had secondaries, I wanted to drop everything and go to Lochcarron. Having cancer hasn't changed Jackie at all, except that he's even more urgent than before to get things done. I suppose being urgent has always described him. If something needed done he wanted it done right away. The strange thing about Jackie's urgency is that he seems to have a great sense of peace at the centre of it. That's always been the case and it's more so now than ever. Cancer has made Jackie more of what he has always been. He has always pushed himself to do things. Now he makes the most of every day.

Marion

The thought of Jackie not being here is a strange one. He took over as father to the family when Dad died and he's always been there for all of us. He wasn't the eldest, but he was the oldest boy at home then. And he's been there for us right through the years. Each year we have an annual family get-together. There were over eighty of us at the last one with three generations of most families there. If Jackie goes before me I'll miss him in all kinds of ways, as a brother and a mentor, and in a way as a father figure too.

Elma

In all the sadness and uncertainty of these last two years I've been so aware of the children's support, and not only that but of their spouses' support too. I count myself richly blessed to have Philip and Marianne, Sarah and Ali, Lois and Donald, Jeremy and Fiona, Jason and Wilma, and I know that I can phone any one of them, children or children-in-law, and know with a certainty that they are there for me. I can say that my best friends are my family, each one playing a different role in my life.

During these months of illness that have stretched into years it's as though I've been held by God, held between his goodness and mercy. I've been at the centre of a goodness and mercy sandwich. That's where David was too. 'Goodness and mercy all my life shall surely follow me: and in God's house for evermore my dwelling place shall be.' That's my past, present and future in a nutshell. God has delivered me, does deliver me and will deliver me – past; present and future are all in God's hands, all part of his goodness and mercy. And in the present I'm glad of whatever deliverance he provides. Elma is being wonderful, and her recent time spent at Strathcarron Hospice and going to some courses there helps her understand me better than I understand myself some of the time. And the doctors and nurses too - I see them as part of God's deliverance for me just now.

My mother used to fret about the grass in the back garden not being cut as often as she'd like. I'd tell her not to worry, that folk knew she wasn't fit to do it. And when someone cut it for her she was so relieved. I didn't understand that then, but I do now. I'm having to learn the lesson I tried to teach her. There are some things I can't any longer do and I've to train myself not to fret about them. As my ability decreases other people have to take them over. Decreasing ability is a strange thing, because it's so up and down. If I've been very sore it can be exciting after the worst has passed just to get up and walk again. I reflect sometimes on what it will be like if things have to be done for me. Over the years I've known folk who needed very basic things done for them and it has moved me to see them accept intimate care with dignity. As I grow nearer to that stage myself, I think that the burden isn't needing help, or getting help, it's being prepared to accept it. Even now, when I'm still able to do most things, I pray that if that times comes I'll be humble enough to accept help with dignity. My dignity isn't to do with external things. It's inside. It's not based on being independent but on the fact that I'm made in God's image. My dignity is because I'm God's child, a prince in the kingdom. I pray that if the day comes when I need basic things done for me I'll see God's good hand in the person who is helping me.

I do think about the prospect of death. There is something unspeakably sad about death and I find it difficult to think about it as anything other than as the Bible describes it, 'the last enemy'. At the same time I know it has been conquered; it's not the end. Death is a fact, the last fact of life. Recently I've found it most distressing when pop stars and others have glamourised death, trying to make it into a joyful occasion, a celebration. That's gruesome. It demeans the fact that Jesus, the Son of God, had to die to destroy death. Even Christians are in danger of doing this and as a result deny themselves the right to grieve. Death is a time of sorrowing but, for the believer, that sorrow is not without hope. There is consolation in sorrow when we are comforted by Christian friends, by God's Word, and by the presence of Christ.

The fact that I'm dying has made me more aware of those with whom I've had serious differences. And it has been lovely that some of these friends have let our differences diminish now that they know I have a terminal illness. That's a little foretaste of heaven for me. We can let differences cause divisions but those of us who are born again are one in Christ Jesus, no matter how many times we divide ourselves into bits and pieces. In heaven it will all be put together and we will rejoice together in praising the God who saved us and washed us from our sins. I get glimpses of that here. Maybe there's someone who thinks what you said or did wasn't right, and because of principles doesn't feel he should have fellowship with you, so he doesn't. But when push comes to shove and you're dying, you both discover that the God-created bond of being one is there, and you love each other. I have had some lovely visits from brothers in Christ whom I haven't seen for years and we have recognised in each other the reality that we are bound together with the Lord our God in what the Bible calls 'the bundle of life'.

I do think about heaven. No more tears, imagine that! The world is a wonderful and amazing place. Even on a wet Lochcarron day it's great to be alive. But there is so much sadness here and I've seen a great amount of it. It'll be great to leave all that behind and especially to be away from all sin, especially my own. I can't begin to take in the wonder of being like Christ. That's what the Bible says we'll be like in heaven. It's a tremendous thought!

13

Goodness and mercy all my life
shall surely follow me:
And in God's house for evermore
my dwelling-place shall be.
(Psalm 23:6)

All That Matters

This book gives me the opportunity to speak as a dying man to men and women who one day must die. That's a preacher's golden opportunity and I can't let it pass.

When I was a boy my grandmother used to come home every year for two weeks, and she joined us in family worship when she was with us. It upset her when Dad prayed for forgiveness. She saw us as a lovely happy family, and because of her generous nature she couldn't see that we'd done anything so serious that we needed to ask God's forgiveness. And I remember Dad, with tears in his eyes, trying to explain to her that he didn't question her sincerity and he didn't doubt her kindness, but that neither would get anyone to heaven, that everyone needed to have their sins forgiven.

I've met some wonderfully sincere people in my life, some even trying sincerely to make amends for things in the past. But no matter how much they try that won't get them to heaven. Sincerity isn't what matters, though many think it is. I've heard it so often - that it doesn't matter what you believe as long as you're sincere. That is not true. Some deeply sincere people are sincerely wrong. What matters is not sincerity but truth. Jesus said, 'I am the way and the truth and the life. No-one comes to the Father except through me' (John 14:6). There is no other way to heaven. The Bible tells us that God is so pure that he can't even look at our sin. Therefore, we certainly can't go to heaven as we are, however sincere. But on the cross Jesus took the punishment for everyone who repents of sin and impurity and who sincerely asks for forgiveness and puts their trust in him. That's the sincerity that matters! 'If we say that we have no sin, we deceive ourselves and the truth is not in us. If we confess our sins, he is faithful and just to forgive us our sins and to cleanse us from all unrighteousness' (1 John 1:8-9). That's why Jesus is the way to heaven – it's because he makes us pure enough to be there. It's amazing, but the Bible says it's true, that when we go to heaven we will be like Jesus.

Many times I've been told by people giving gifts to Blythswood that, 'Whatever you do for the least of people you do for Jesus'. It has alarmed me that they seemed to be trusting in what they were doing rather than on what Christ did at Calvary. But it's only through Christ we can be saved. Salvation is all of grace. We can do nothing to deserve it, even if we spend our whole lives trying to do good. The Bible says that 'all our righteous acts are like filthy rags' (Isaiah 64:6). Good deeds are not the way to heaven. Jesus said, 'For God so loved the world that he gave his one and only Son, that whoever believes in him shall not perish but have eternal life' (John 3:16). It's not our good deeds that make the difference – it's what Jesus did on the cross.

As a young man I tried hard to get close to Christ, but I was trying in my own strength. I thought that self-discipline and church attendance could get me to him and I tried harder and harder but got nowhere. Then I gave up. Finally it dawned on me that I was complicating Christianity. All I needed was faith in Christ and dependence on him alone. We can't get away from, 'Believe on the Lord Jesus Christ and you will be saved.' We're afraid of that today. It's too simple. But it needs to be said over and over and over again. There is no hope otherwise. If you are struggling in your own strength to get to Jesus, stop struggling and trust him. He's done all that's necessary. Believe on him and be saved.

I've met people who thought that their sins were too big to be forgiven. But Jesus came to save big sinners. Christ is bigger than all our sins, and he died for us knowing what we are and what we're like. A few months ago, in an article in a newspaper, I said that repentance is urgent. A man phoned from a hotel when he read it. He said that his life was in a terrible mess. He was in the hotel with a woman who wasn't his wife and he was an incurable gambler too. I asked if there was a Gideon Bible in his room. There was. I told him to look in the index for Confession and to read the passage it pointed him too. 'Do I have to tell God everything?' he asked. I told him that it was certainly good to confess all our sins, but that God knew them all already. He knows everything about us. There was a tremendous sigh at the end of the phone. 'That's a relief,' the man said. 'That means I can come to him.' That man knew he was a big sinner and that he'd forgotten most of the sins he'd committed. He knew he couldn't confess all his sins individually because he couldn't remember the half of them. So if you were to say to me that you're too big a sinner to be forgiven, I'd tell you that God is a bigger God than you're a big sinner, and that the way is open for you to come.

Many people wonder how they can know they're forgiven. The Bible tells us that Jesus is the Truth. He cannot lie. If God's Word says that those who confess their sins are forgiven then that's that. There's no arguing with God.

Others who sympathised with me because my cancer was incurable have died before me and completely unexpectedly. If you haven't already cast yourself on Jesus' mercy, don't delay. He's waiting and he's willing to forgive and accept you. And I promise that if you come to him he'll surround you with his goodness and his mercy for the rest of your life. I know, because he's done it for me. The other certainty for the believer is that he will be in heaven, God's house, for ever more. And that becomes more precious to me day by day as the end of my life here on earth draws near.

14

Thou wilt me shew the path of life:
of joys there is full store
Before thy face; at thy right hand
are pleasures evermore.
(Psalm 16:11)

The Final Chapter

by Philip Ross

At ten minutes past midnight on Wednesday the thirteenth of March 2002, my father died. That struggle on into the first ten minutes of another day seemed to reflect his spirit of determination. Yet he did not die as a man desperately trying to hold on to life.

During his illness he embraced pain, refusing to reduce his workload because of unpleasant treatment unless he had no choice. But at the end of February, when the doctors told him that they could do no more, he accepted that with calmness. Not that he 'gave up,' but with his remaining energy, he focused on the world to come and encouraged others to do the same. Although he felt no sudden need to prepare himself – Christ had done that – the nearness of death brought heaven into sharper view.

In these first two weeks of March friends came to visit him for the last time. 'He's a covenant-keeping God,' was what he had to tell them. It was also his message to his own children. At the heart of the new covenant is the promise, 'They shall be my people, and I will be their God; then I will give them one heart and one way, that they may fear me forever, for the good of them and their children after them. And I will make an everlasting covenant with them, that I will not turn away from doing them good; but I will put my fear in their hearts so that they will not depart from me' (Jeremiah 32:38-40). In his own experience he knew God as one who kept that promise. His prayer for us was that 'they may not be like their fathers, a stubborn and rebellious generation, a generation that did not set its heart aright, and whose spirit was not faithful to God' (Psalm 78:8). And he was sure that God's covenant love extended to his children's children too.

If he had any concern in these last few days it was that he had 'not been plain enough with people' about their need to turn away from sin and to trust in Christ for mercy. That is why he wanted us to find a copy of something Blythswood had published many years earlier by Adolphe Monod which could be reprinted and distributed after his death. All our searching for the original publication was fruitless until my sister, Sarah, found what he had in mind in a book of French sermons. She translated the extract for him, but it required some introduction, and that is what led to him writing what was entitled 'My Last Letter' in the last week of his life. The message was simple, 'We all need Christ; without him, we will perish.'

His last conversations were on Sunday evening, although during the night he would still quote the words of resurrection hope from Psalm 17, 'But as for me, I thine own face in righteousness will see; and with thy likeness, when I wake, I satisfied shall be.' Jan van Woerden came on the Tuesday. Reminding him of the words in Psalm 68, 'God's chariots twenty thousand are, thousands of angels strong,' Jan told him that one of God's chariots would come for him shortly. Within twelve hours, he was away.

No other parting could be more drawn out, and yet so sudden. Family bonds are a lifetime in the making, a moment in the breaking. We experienced the shocking truth of the words we would sing a few days later at the funeral service, 'Thou dost unto destruction man that is mortal turn; and unto them thou say'st, Again, ye sons of men, return.'

Then came an outpouring of sympathy – hundreds of cards and letters, including many unexpected messages of genuine respect. There was the strange experience of reading the news of his death and obituaries in the newspapers. The writer in *The Herald* determined that 'as a preacher he was unremarkable.' Although only the Judge who has all the evidence can make that assessment, my father would have agreed even had he written, 'As a minister, as a Christian, or as a man, he was unremarkable.' On his deathbed he could only describe himself, with the kind of sincerity unique to a dying man, as an 'unprofitable servant.'

The following week the funeral service was held in Dingwall Free Church. Presenting a tribute, Alexander Murray quoted Samuel Rutherford, 'Oh, well it is forever, Oh, well for evermore,' and certainly we could not have wished him back to 'this death-doomed shore.' Levente Horváth prayed for successors who would give God no rest and no peace until he would make the church a praise in the earth. In his address to the congregation, George Macaskill picked up on the words we sung from Psalm 118, 'I shall not die but live, and shall the works of God discover.'

The church was full. I had never seen so many people in a church building in this country. But the crowd would soon disperse and only one task would remain for us as far as my father was concerned: to carry him to his grave. So we returned to Locharron where, below cloudless skies and snow-capped hills, we buried John Walter Ross.

The sympathy of all those who joined us was sincere, yet, in all that kindness there was an indefinable emptiness – a death-shaped void – that we could not fill. But we were not without hope. We knew that there was a more glorious world, far surpassing the beauty that surrounded us, and soon the grave that we had filled would be empty again. We could hear Jesus saying, 'Surely I come quickly,' and we were saying, 'Even so, come, Lord Jesus.'

Leaving the burial ground, we passed the graves of Lachlan MacLeod and Angus Mackay, both at one time Free Presbyterian ministers with my father. Like him, they were not enthusiastic combatants in ecclesiastical wars, but all that was behind them now. No more strife. No more tears.

Some said that day, 'It's the end of an era.' To what extent that is true is not yet known. Many people told us, by letter or in person, that my father had helped them by giving them work in Blythswood when in their own estimation they were unremarkable, or even less than unremarkable. But such people have made Blythswood what it is and that era should not end. It was his constant concern that weak and insecure people would find a place within the organisation, and that it would be led by more than the 'not many' (1 Cor. 1:26-29). For as long as the gospel is the driving force, Blythswood will bear witness to the crucified Christ in that way.

It is perhaps more likely that his passing coincides with the ending of an era in the church. Of his contemporaries, he is one of the first to move on. When he began his ministry the scene in the Highlands was very different. Most villages had two or three well-attended congregations, with ministers to lead them. Thirty years on many church buildings are almost empty and the remaining ministers look after several congregations. It appears that the institutions of 150 years or more are guttering to an end. Yet we hope that in all that the Lord of the vineyard is pruning rather than destroying.

We do have reason to hope. In God's giving of his Son and in the gift of his Spirit we see the measure of his goodwill towards his people in every age. Whatever changes may accompany the rise and fall of generations, we know that the era of his lovingkindness will not end.

'He gives his people strength and power. Blessed be God.'

My Last Letter

(Written by Jackie Ross shortly before he died with the instruction that it be distributed at his funeral service.)

9 March 2002

Dear friend,

My life is almost at an end. By the time that you read this, I will be in heaven. In these last days, I have been convinced that I was not always plain enough with people during my life. We all need Christ; without him, we will perish. Yet, it can be difficult even to ask your own family, 'Are you really trusting in Christ?'

At this point, it is hard for me to put more than one sentence together, but somehow I want to say what could not easily be said, and what should have been said.

Many of you have wilfully rejected Christ. Your conscience convicts you and you know that you will give an account, but you suppress the truth. Friends and all as we have been, I must say that you will not get away with that. You are without excuse. You need to trust in Christ; without him, you will perish.

We all need Christ. It is easy for us to be self-righteous hypocrites, even looking for opportunities to point out that other people are self-righteous. But that will not do. We cannot depend on any thing that we do. We all need Christ, and all we need is Christ.

Someone has translated this extract for me from the sermons of the French preacher, Adolphe Monod. He says here what I would like to say to you myself.

Faith, not works; that is the gospel. That is what distinguishes it from all human systems. All the doctrines conceived by man and all the false interpretations given to the doctrines of God by religions throughout the ages say to sinners, 'Do this or do that and you will live.' Sacrifice your life, your health or your well-being, throw yourself under the wheels of a juggernaut, sit on the ground, hold your arm outstretched until it grows stiff and withers, keep silence for the rest of your days and your sins will be forgiven. Do penance, go on a long pilgrimage, withdraw from society and bury yourself in sad solitude, fast, abstain from things, mutilate yourself, crucify yourself and your sins will be forgiven. Do good works, help the poor, visit sick people, fight your temptations, be sober, just, without reproach and your sins will be forgiven.

How different is the language of the gospel! Believe! Stop being consumed with fruitless efforts to work your own reconciliation with God. You will never ever succeed. A way to be saved is still available to you but it is by completely giving up hope in yourself.

It is in crying to God, 'Grace, grace, be merciful to me a sinner,' 'It is by grace you have been saved, through faith – and this not from yourselves, it is the gift of God – not by works, so that no one can boast.' No matter who you are it is by faith you can be saved.

But what do you have to believe?

'Believe on the Lord Jesus Christ and you will be saved.' 'Believe in the Lord Jesus Christ' is a phrase you will have heard so often, maybe even repeated it many times yourself, perhaps since you were a little child, so that it hardly even occurs to you that you could do with it being explained. It is so simple that even a child can understand it and that is perhaps partly why most people don't understand it.

'Believe on the Lord Jesus Christ.' Do you really understand this? Place all hope for your salvation in him. Build on him. Do not be afraid to lean on him. He is the Rock of Ages. Believe in Jesus Christ. Dwell in him. Clothe yourself in him. Believe in the Lord Jesus Christ then, and you will be saved.

Consider this my friend, because you will follow me soon enough.

Yours sincerely

John Walter Ross

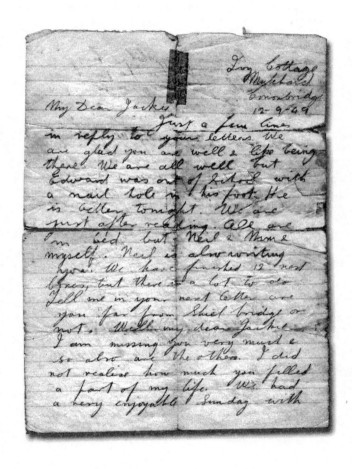

Hand written letter from Jackie's dad to Jackie when he left home.
See pages 26-7

questions & answers I wished you were with but I am glad you are happy there & it will not be long now untill Xmas Have Confidence in Christ & what he did for us

subject on Sunday Edward asked some peculiar questions but we got him put right and indeed it was all very edifying. Remember your prayers & the things you were taught here at home. Remember him who is all things to you that is good for you & who gave His all for you. Keep always remembering them. Talk often to Him. Tell Him all your sins, & your troubles. Remember He died for you He is your best & most powerfull friend Jackie. Draw near to Him Jackie & He will draw near to you my boy. Till the Eternal day dawn & the shadows flee away Jackie try harder & harder to draw nearer to Him who desires your Salvation so much that he died for you I hope you will get on well. With love from Dad

201

For more information about the work Blythswood is
involved in, they can be contacted at the following address.

Blythswood Care,
Deephaven,
Evanton,
Ross-shire
Scotland
United Kingdom
IV16 9XJ

Tel: +44 (0)1349 830777
Fax: +44 (0)1349 830477
E-mail: info@blythswood.org
www.blythswood.org

Other Books of interest
from Christian Focus

David Livingstone
The Truth Behind The Legend
Rob Mackenzie

An easy and absorbing read... Quite a man. Quite a heart. Quite a book. **The Mercury**

A man of whom the human race can be justly proud. He shows us that courage, determination and faith are more than a match for life's great challenges. **Bob Edmiston, Chairman, International Motors Group**

Livingstone, perhaps the best known missionary of them all. The story of a poor lad from Scotland whose attempts to find the source of the Nile and famous meeting with Henry Morton Stanley have become the stuff of legend.

The truth behind the legend, however, is even more compelling. Drawing extensively from Livingstone's personal notes and letters, Rob Mackenzie unfolds the intensely human story of a man with a vision – to set souls free from slavery, both physically and spiritually, and to open up Africa to Christianity and lawful commerce.

Livingstone's life has come to be purely based on a few events, lost in legend, yet his tomb inscription reads

'Brought by faithful hands over land and sea, here rests David Livingstone. Missionary, Traveller, Philanthropist... for 30 years his life was spent in an unwearied effort to evangelise the native races, to explore the undiscovered secrets, to abolish the desolating slave trade of Central Africa where with his last words he wrote *"all I can add in my solitude, is, may heaven's rich blessing come down on every one, American, English, or Turk, who will help to heal this open sore of the world."*

What caused him to become such a well-loved figure, and to attempt such immense tasks?

An amazing story awaits you upon turning the first page

ISBN 1 85792 6153

That Man of Granite with the Heart of a Child
A New Biography of J. C. Ryle
Eric Russell

It is very good to have Ryle's story told afresh by someone who understands it so well...Ryle was an Anglican to remember. **J. I. Packer**

John Charles Ryle was born into a comfortable English family background - his father was a politician and businessman. Ryle was intelligent, a great sportsman (captain of cricket at Eton and Oxford) and was set for a career in his father's business, and then politics – a typical, well to do, 19th century family.

Then – disaster. The family awoke to find that their father's bank had failed, taking all the other businesses with it. Ryle had lost his job and his place in society. He resigned his commission in the local yeomanry and went to comfort his parents, brother and sisters. One moment a popular man with good prospects, the next the son of a bankrupt with no trade or profession.

Almost as a last resort, he was ordained into the ministry of the church. Who could have thought that such an uninspiring entry into the ministry could have such an impact on the spiritual life of a nation.

Ryle's reputation as a pastor and leader grew until he was appointed the first Bishop of Liverpool, a post he held for 20 years. He was an author who is still in print today (he put aside royalties to pay his father's debts) and a man once described by his successor as 'that man of granite with the heart of a child.' He changed the face of the English church.

Ryle stands as a colossus at the junction of two centuries – a hundred years after his death he still stands as an example to church leaders today of how to combine leadership, a firm faith and compassion.

Eric Russell was ordained as a Church of England minister but is better known as a college lecturer training teachers in Religious Studies. He has previously written about the history of the Liverpool diocese.

ISBN 1 85792 6315

It is not Death to Die
A New biography of Hudson Taylor
Jim Cromarty

Hudson Taylor's philosophy was simple

'There is a living God,
He has spoken in the Bible.
He means what he says,
and will do all that he has promised.'

Hudson Taylor's life is one that should encourage Christians to step out in faith to fulfil the commands of God. His life's work was motivated by a love of God and a love of his fellow man. His heart's desire was to see Christ glorified in people coming to faith, particularly the Chinese.

Encouraged by another missionary, W.C. Burns, Hudson changed western dress and imperialistic attitudes for Chinese ways. He served, and still serves, as a model for mission work around the world.

He led an extraordinary life and Jim Cromarty has succeeded in capturing the thrill of his pioneering work. It is as if we too are able to step outside the comfortable boundaries most of us never come close to exploring beyond.

If you have enjoyed reading about Hudson Taylor then see also Hudson Taylor's Legacy (ISBN 1 85792 4924) edited by Marshall Broomhall, Hudson and Maria (ISBN 1 85792 2239) by John Pollock, God's Polished Arrow: the life of W.C. Burns (ISBN 1 85792 3952) by Michael McMullen and, for children, Hudson Taylor - An Adventure Begins (ISBN 1 85792 4231) by Catherine Mackenzie.

Jim Cromarty is an Australian minister and has written other successful biographies and family devotional books.

ISBN 1 85792 6323

Fire in My Bones
A Story of Pioneering Mission in Africa
Dick Anderson

Dick Anderson's story makes astonishing reading. He and his wife, Joan, were pioneering missionaries in Turkana, Kenya, spending many years in the front line of world evangelisation. Their ground-breaking experiences were used by Africa Inland Mission (AIM) to evaluate the possibility of mission the length and breadth of Africa. But this is not just another story of missionary success, Dick critically reviews his work at the mission in Turkana, and evaluates how the mission has progressed since they it began in the late fifties.

'Dick Anderson hides nothing of the risks, the privations faced, the impact on his wife and family, and the deep personal struggles he went through. This is a 'must read' for those who feel called to take the gospel to unreached peoples.'
Rev Tom Houston

'This book is the testimony of one of those in whose heart has burned the passion of Paul for those as yet denied access to the message of the gospel. If this book kindles such a fire in the bones of some of the Lord's people – it will have served its purpose well.' **John Brand, Africa Inland Mission**

No one reading this biography will remain unchallenged. It is a thrilling and gripping account of risks undertaken and dangers faced for the sake of the Gospel.' **Timothy G Alford**

'The Andersons have a remarkable story to tell covering quite the most exciting and challenging period of Africa's encounter with the Gospel.'
Patrick Johnstone, WEC, Author of Operation World

ISBN 1 85792 676 5

God's Polished Arrow
W. C. Burns - Revival Preacher
Dr. Michael McMullen

William Chalmers Burns was surrounded by revival. Not only was he used by God in Scotland, Continental Europe and North America, but he was also a pioneer missionary in China (Where he persuaded a young man called Hudson Taylor to dress in Chinese clothes). His Journals were important and valuable as a first hand account of revival and as a record of a man's life singularly used by God.

Burns was used mightily of God in his native Scotland but turned his back on the acclaim gained from revival to respond to the passion of his life, sharing the gospel in China. Burns sacrificed material comforts, suffered illness and harassment, and labored unto death in order bring the good news of Jesus Christ to the interior of China. This unique biography by Dr. Michael McMullen, including Burns' letters, sermons and journal entries, will be an inspiration and blessing to all who read it and a model for those in the twenty-first century. **Jerry Rankin, President, International Mission Board, Southern Baptist Convention**

Sometimes while reading stirring biography I wonder why I read anything else. The life of W.C. Burns falls into this category. Few men have seen more of the Lord's evident blessing on their preaching than Burns. Fewer still have seen such dramatic results both in their own homeland and among previously unreached peoples. **Dr. Don Whitney, Associate Professor of Spiritual Formation, Midwestern Baptist Theological Seminary**

... warmly presents the whole of this godly man's revival preaching and missionary zeal. God's Polished Arrow is about the sacrifices and massive affect of an eminently holy man. **Jim Elliff, Midwestern Center for Biblical Revival, Kansas City, Missouri**

Dr. Michael McMullen is Professor of Church History at Midwestern Baptist Seminary, Kansas City. He has previously edited The Passionate Preacher, previously unpublished sermons of Robert Murray McCheyne' ISBN 1 85792 410X

ISBN 1 85792 3952

From Whitewashed Stairs to Heaven

Maureen McKenna and 'Open Doors Trust Glasgow'

Maureen McKenna with Irene Howat

A promising national swimmer, Maureen McKenna, has to stop the sport she loves on medical grounds. She is determined to fight back but a combination of commercial acumen and problem drinking sees her repeatedly soar and crash until Maureen becomes an alcoholic. But then an amazing story unfolds. She meets Hugh at Alcoholics Anonymous and becomes a Christian. They marry and work with homeless people, prostitutes and addicts in the streets of Glasgow until, realising that the people they help need more than food and clothes, they set up Open Door Trust Glasgow to break the cycle of deprivation..

This is a challenging book which should encourage Christians to get out into the market place and share their faith and works with those most in need. **Sir David McNee, Retired Commissioner, Metropolitan Police**

Maureen McKenna's life story breathes the air of the two worlds in which she has lived. The Glasgow in which she was born and whose people she so obviously loves, and the Kingdom of God... A great read! **Rev. Sinclair Ferguson, St. George's Tron Church, Glasgow**

Government policies and urban renewal schemes can change the environment, fund organisations, and create opportunities. But only God can change people. And he does. If you doubt that, read on! **John Nicholls, London City Mission**

A window into both the heart of God and his power to change lives. **Laspic Stewart, Chairman, Open Door Trust Glasgow**

Once, like us all, a prisoner of sin, Maureen McKenna and her husband Hugh, now reach others who are still trapped. This is a compelling book. **Rev. Jackie Ross, Blythswood Christian Care**

ISBN 1 85792 6161